It Happened by Design

It Happened by Design

The Life and Work of Arthur Q. Davis

Arthur Q. Davis, FAIA

Introductory essay by J. Richard Gruber

University Press of Mississippi in association with

The Ogden Museum of Southern Art, University of New Orleans

www.upress.state.ms.us

The University Press of Mississippi is a member of the
Association of American University Presses.

Page ii: Rivergate Convention Center, New Orleans, Louisiana. Photo-
graph by Frank Lotz Miller
Page viii: Louisiana State Penitentiary, Angola. Photograph by Frank
Lotz Miller

Illustrations on pages ii, viii, 67, 71–72, 73, 75–76, 77, 81, 82–83,
94–95, 97 (top), 98–101, 104–7, 109–10, 116 (top and bottom right),
122–23, 126–27, 128–29, 130, 132, and 133 are courtesy of Southeastern Architectural Archive, Special Collections Division, Tulane
University Libraries, Curtis & Davis Office Records. Illustrations on
pages 68, 69, 78, 79, 80, 84, 89–92, 111, 112–13, and 124 are courtesy
of Tulane School of Architecture, Visual Resources Library. All other
illustrations are courtesy of Arthur Q. Davis, unless otherwise cred-
ited.

Library of Congress Cataloging-in-Publication Data
Davis, Arthur Q.
   It happened by design : the life and work of Arthur Q. Davis / Ar-
thur Q. Davis ; introductory essay by J. Richard Gruber.
      p. cm.
   Includes bibliographical references.
   ISBN 978-1-60473-265-8 (cloth : alk. paper) 1. Davis, Arthur
Q. 2. Architects—United States—Biography. 3. International
style (Architecture)—Gulf Coast (U.S.) 4. International style
(Architecture)—Louisiana—New Orleans. I. Gruber, J. Richard. II.
Title.
   NA737.D335A2 2009
   720.92—dc22
   [B]   2008049850

British Library Cataloging-in-Publication Data available

This is dedicated to

James M. Davis and Juanita Davis

Mary Davis

Quint Davis

Pamela Davis Friedler

Jill Davis Botnick

Acknowledgments

In many respects, this book and the related exhibition at the Ogden Museum of Southern Art began many decades ago, when Arthur Davis, then fourteen years old, discovered architecture through the hands of a skilled New Orleans mason who was constructing a fireplace, as detailed in a set of blueprints, for a house being built near Audubon Park. Thanks to that mason, and those architect's blueprints (the first Davis had seen), the interest of a future architect was sparked. Three years later, at the age of seventeen, he was enrolled in the School of Architecture at Tulane University.

Since that time, many individuals have encouraged the evolution of his career and this project. Arthur Davis would like to thank the following people who made significant contributions to the preparation of this book: Stephen Ambrose, Sarah Cloonan, Val Dansereau, Mary Davis, Quint Davis, Pam Davis Friedler, Milly Hockingheimer, Rosemary James, Karen Kingsley, Ann Konigsmark, Reed Kroloff, Kathy Driscoll Lopez, Heather Skeehan, Francine Stock, and Bonnie Warren.

On behalf of the Ogden Museum, I also would like to thank Francine Stock of the Tulane Architectural Archives for her research on this project, as well as Dr. Keli Rylance, Director of the Southeastern Architectural Archives at Tulane University (home to the Curtis and Davis archives and the Arthur Q. Davis archives). The photographs used in this book reflect the deep holdings of these archives, especially those of Frank Lotz Miller, a significant architectural photographer who is featured in this book. We thank his heirs for permission to reproduce his images and the opportunity to bring them to wider recognition. We also thank all of the photographers featured in the book, including Richard Sexton, whose sensitive images of specific New Orleans projects, completed in 2008, reflect their post-Katrina condition (for better and worse) in the book's epilogue.

This publication reflects an ongoing publishing partnership between the Ogden Museum of Southern Art, University of New Orleans, and the University Press of Mississippi. Special thanks are owed to Seetha Srinivasan, long-term (and now retired) director of the Press, for her support of the project, and to her successor, Leila Salisbury, who embraced the project after coming to the Press as its new director. Thanks also to Anne Stascavage for her sensitive editing, to Walter Biggins for shepherding the project to completion, and to John Langston for his outstanding design work and his sensitivity to Arthur Davis's architectural legacy and the architectural heritage of New Orleans.

At the Ogden Museum of Southern Art, thanks to Elaine LaCour and to David Houston, Jan Katz, Bradley Sumrall, Sue Strachan, Kate Barron, Richard McCabe, and Michael Barr.

And finally, we express our appreciation to all of those individuals, agencies, and organizations working in post-Katrina New Orleans who document and preserve the architecture and the built environment of this city and the larger Gulf Coast region (including some of the projects featured in this book).

JRG

Contents

In 2007, the Ogden Museum of Southern Art hosted an exhibition titled "Regional Modernism," organized by the New Orleans chapter of the American Institute of Architects (AIA), which brought renewed attention to the modernist legacy of Arthur Q. Davis and Nathaniel Curtis Jr. and their firm, Curtis and Davis. Later in 2007, during a series of ongoing conversations with me, Arthur Davis brought the working manuscript for this publication to my attention. After reading it and discussing it with Davis, I began to explore ways to publish the book, working ultimately in partnership with the University Press of Mississippi, leading to the publication of the current volume.

During the spring and summer of 2008, as the third anniversary of Hurricane Katrina approached, Arthur Davis reflected upon his career in New Orleans, witnessing the evolving nature of his professional legacy in the city of his birth. Then, ironically, in late August of 2008, Hurricane Gustav moved toward New Orleans, forcing a massive evacuation of the city and the cancellation of many Katrina memorial services. Davis and his family evacuated to an historic house in Natchez, Mississippi, where they watched televised images, along with the rest of the nation, to see if New Orleans would survive.

New Orleans did survive, damaged by wind and impacted by massive power losses, and Davis returned in early September, just in time to consider another evacuation as Hurricane Ike formed rapidly and moved toward New Orleans. Ike's course shifted toward western Louisiana and the Texas coast, then hit Galveston and Houston. As these events underscore, the publication of this book, focused on Davis's professional and personal memoirs, and the organization of a related exhibition at the Ogden Museum, reflect the conditions evident in a specific time and place—post-Katrina, and now post-Gustav, New Orleans—and the significance of Davis's career within that context, including the demolition and rebuilding that mark life in the Crescent City.

Arthur Davis and his family celebrated his eighty-eighth birthday this March in the city where he was born and raised. An alert and engaging man who remains attuned to the daily life of New Orleans, he has seen many projects and key elements of his modernist vision for the city disappear in a relatively short time span. The fate of many remaining Gulf Coast churches, schools, and public buildings still hang in the balance, at the mercy of political forces, FEMA policies, and federal rebuilding initiatives—and the next hurricane in the Gulf of Mexico. Recently, while studying the abandoned and decaying state of his firm's George Washington Carver High School campus, a modernist landmark located near the Industrial Canal and the Ninth Ward of New Orleans, Davis repeated a phrase I hear increasingly often. "An architect should not outlive his work."

In contrast, and to Davis's pleasure, the Louisiana Superdome, an architectural icon of New Orleans and the Curtis and Davis firm, one recognized around the world—and one that became a heavily damaged, endangered symbol of failed government and human suffering after Katrina—has been restored (costing over $180 million) and returned to public use (on September 25, 2006, with a New Orleans Saints football game). The Louisiana Superdome, and its neighbor, the New Orleans Arena (designed by Davis), serve as dominant symbols of the city's recovery, achieving iconic stature again in the twenty-first century—hosting conventions and public events, as well as the revived New Orleans Saints and New Orleans Hornets sports programs.

For six decades, Davis and his partners—in firms including Curtis and Davis and Arthur Q. Davis FAIA and Partners—advanced modern architecture, adapting and refining international design trends to reflect the materials, environment, and traditions of specific regions. As Davis's text indicates, this was never a provincial endeavor. At its peak, for example, the Curtis and Davis firm (1947–1978) maintained offices in New Orleans as well as in New York, Los Angeles, London, and Berlin. In 1978, the Curtis and Davis firm merged with a California architectural and engineering firm, Daniel, Mann, Johnson and Mendenhall (DMJM). Davis became a vice president, operating its New Orleans office under the name DMJM Curtis & Davis. Curtis parted ways with Davis then, deciding to open his own firm, Nathaniel Curtis, FAIA, Architect, in 1978 and maintained this practice until his death in 1997. After ten years with DMJM, Davis opened Arthur Q. Davis FAIA and Partners in New Orleans, working on local projects including the New Orleans Arena as well as international projects like the creation of Kuala Kencana, a new town in Indonesia.

The number of national and international buildings associated with Davis's career is significant, including the United States Embassy in Saigon, the James V. Forrestal Federal Office Building in Washington, the Medical Center Free University of Berlin, West Germany, and numerous hotels, hospitals, and commercial structures across the world. In New Orleans and the state of Louisiana, projects include the Louisiana Superdome; the New Orleans Arena; the Rivergate (demolished); the UNO Keifer Lakefront Arena and UNO campus master plan; Louisiana State Penitentiary at Angola; the Royal Sonesta and Royal Orleans hotels in the French Quarter; schools including Thomy Lafon Elementary, George Washington Carver High School, and St. Francis Cabrini High School (demolished); the New Orleans Public Library; and many other schools, churches, office buildings, and residential structures.

Advancing modernism in New Orleans was not an easy task initially, especially in a city so deeply rooted in architectural history and tradition. Davis and his partners regularly fought resistance to modern design, especially in public projects. After working for more than sixty years to create a modern legacy and environment, Davis watched that environment change overnight after Hurricane Katrina passed over the Gulf Coast. Now, Katrina's impact upon the Gulf Coast South—what has survived, what has not, and what remains endangered—offers an opportunity to consider an important modernist legacy, the impact one architect and his partners have had upon a city and region over six decades, and how that influence was reflected in international projects in diverse climatic and social environments.

This essay offers an overview, reflecting the historical and social context for the projects and ideas presented in this book by Arthur Davis, primarily focusing on New Orleans and the Gulf Coast South. Many of the architect's national and international projects were based upon, or influenced by, projects created and refined in the Gulf Coast region. Now, as New Orleans and the Gulf Coast continue to recover and rebuild in the post-Katrina (and post-Gustav) era, the importance of these projects and the progressive architectural and social vision associated with them stands as an important legacy, one that should not be lost, or overlooked, in the rush to rebuild a major American city.

When Arthur Davis was born in New Orleans, on March 30, 1920, the city was more closely tied to the nineteenth century than to the twentieth century. Its French Quarter changed little after the turn of the century and in the years after World War One. Artists and writers embraced the French Quarter then as a bastion of the old orders, a creative and historic remnant, not unlike Paris. To many it served as the American version of that cultural capitol. During the years of Davis's boyhood noted cultural figures came to the city, including William Faulkner and Sherwood Anderson, while others, including Louis Armstrong and other jazz musicians, left to seek opportunities in the cities of the North.

Sherwood Anderson described the allure of the French Quarter in 1922, two years after Arthur Davis's birth. "At the present moment I am living in New Orleans, I have a room in the 'Vieux Carre,' with long French windows, through which one can step out upon a gallery, as wide as the street below." After recounting the leisurely pace of his working process, he described the city outside his windows, in romantic terms. "There is an old city here, on the lip of America, as it were, and all about it has been built a new and more modern city. In the old city a people once lived who loved to play, who made love in the moonlight, who walked under trees, gambled with death in the dueling fields."[1]

In a remarkable coincidence, Davis's life, spanning the twentieth and twenty-first centuries, has been bracketed by two of the most significant natural and manmade disasters in the nation's history—both related to New Orleans, to the Mississippi River, and to flooding of historic proportions. Shortly after his seventh birthday, Davis and his family witnessed the power and destruction of the Mississippi River as the city, and the lower Mississippi River valley, were threatened by the great floods of 1927. New Orleans ultimately survived the flood, but the Davis family lost properties nearby in Point-a-La-Hache, Louisiana, as a result of this disaster. It was an event that taught the young Davis lasting lessons—about the river, the importance of engineering and levee systems, the control of levee boards, and the role of government agencies—long before 2005, when Hurricanes Katrina and Rita radically altered the built environment of Louisiana and the Gulf Coast.[2]

Davis came of age during the Great Depression, while New Orleans struggled with the rest of the nation, yet maintained its unique pace despite the economic crisis. His family circumstances were not severely affected by the Depression, making it possible for him to attend one of New Orleans's best schools, Isadore Newman Manual and Training School, located near the University and Audubon Park neighborhoods where he lived. His mother and her brothers, who had also moved to New Orleans, opened and operated a department store on Canal Street, The Emporium, which the young Davis loved to visit on a regular basis, absorbing the colors, sounds, and energies of Canal Street, the city's business and commercial center. An only child, he recalls spending many hours alone, often riding his bike, exploring Uptown neighborhoods and Audubon Park, which he recalls as more "primitive and raw" in those years, qualities he enjoyed.

When he was fourteen, as he writes, a singular encounter convinced him that he should become an architect—his discovery of architectural blueprints and the power of architectural drawing—when he passed a brick mason laying a wall near Audubon Park, following the exact instructions contained in the drawing. Not long after, rather remarkably it seems, while he was still a high school student, Davis obtained a summer job in an architectural office—with the important Louisiana firm, Weiss, Dreyfuss & Seifert—working on the drawings for the new Art Deco Louisiana Capitol building, a favorite project of legendary Governor Huey P. Long. And, as he describes, Huey Long stopped to speak to him during the governor's visits to that office.

At the age of seventeen (after graduation from Newman), following his dream with singular focus, Davis enrolled in the School of Architecture at Tulane University, in a program he recalls being rooted in French Beaux-Arts architectural traditions. Though his text makes little reference to it, and despite the economic impact of the Depression, Davis was exposed to a surprising range of architectural and engineering development in New Orleans and across the state as a result of Roosevelt-era federal programs and Long-era state plans. Among the federal projects of the Public Works Administration were the building of a new Charity Hospital in New Orleans (damaged and closed since Katrina, and a cause for preservationists now), rebuilding the historic French Market, and expansive infrastructure work on the New Orleans sewer, water, and storm drainage systems. In addition to Huey Long's state capitol building, state projects united parts of Louisiana with new paved roads (the Airline Highway from New Orleans to Baton Rouge, for example) and massive bridges (the Huey P. Long Bridge in New Orleans), and provided such facilities as schools, university structures, government buildings, airports, stadium facilities, and hospitals.[3]

The federal government also supported artists, writers, and performers through its programs in New Orleans, including the Federal Writers' Project of the Works Progress Administration. Directed by New Orleans writer Lyle Saxon, the *New Orleans City Guide* (1938) offered observations about the city's architecture when Davis was a student at Tulane. "The United States has few cities wherein the architecture of their original inhabitants has left a permanent stamp of distinctiveness and individuality. New Orleans is one of them." After describing the French Quarter, the Garden District, and notable public buildings in detail, the guide's writers made only passing reference to contemporary architecture in the city. "Of strictly modern architecture New Orleans has but few examples. The most recent of its skyscrapers are the Hibernia, American, and Canal Banks, and the Pere Marquette Building. Possibly the closest approximation to what is now considered modern architecture is the Shushan Airport's administration building."[4]

Writers in the guide also described significant cultural influences evident in New Orleans in 1938 (still evident in 2008). Lingering evidence of the slave trade and the city's ties to African and Caribbean cultures were found in musical and spiritual traditions, including voodoo, which merited specific reference. "Congo Square (now Beauregard Square) was given over to slaves on Sunday afternoons for dancing, singing, and the performance of Voodoo rites. As long as Negroes were imported as slaves, the old religions were kept alive. With the end of slave traffic and as a result of constant proselytism, the Negro transferred his emotionalism to Christian creeds; but Voodooism and other primitive rituals have persisted in various forms down to the present."[5]

As a native son, and as described in his text, the influence of voodoo was evident during Davis's early years in New Orleans. Voodoo was represented in symbols he discovered in the French Quarter while working on an architectural assignment at Tulane, "mounds of powdered red brick dust and white substances drawn in patterns," marking his initial encounter with voodoo practices. A more profound encounter with voodoo came when an older black worker under his supervision at the Delta Shipbuilding Company gave him a "mojo" for protection after he enlisted in the navy, which he describes as a "small red oilcloth packet about the size of a large postage stamp, which had been handstitched." Davis carried this, protecting it (as it protected him, he believes) throughout his war experiences. Later in his career, he expanded his knowledge of voodoo on a working trip to Haiti, an experience he still describes with high regard.

While in architectural school at Tulane, Davis met his wife, Mary Henriette Wineman, a student from Detroit then studying at Newcomb College. After he completed his fifth year of architectural study at Tulane, they were married, on August 30, 1942. Mary completed her degree later at Newcomb, focusing on literature and dance. Soon after their wedding, Davis received a position with an influential architect in Detroit, working on Albert Kahn's staff with a team of structural engineers, before he was sent back to New Orleans, where he was involved in supervising engineering and construction standards on flying boats. Not content with this support activity during a time of war, he enlisted in the navy, serving as an officer with the Department of Ship Camouflage, where he advanced camouflage painting on naval vessels in the Pacific theater. Still fascinated by these experiences, he continues to study declassified documents from his naval service and recently presented a lecture on camouflage techniques to a New Orleans military group, accompanied by Mary and his son Quint and daughter Pam.

Following his service and travels during World War II, and his working experiences with Albert Kahn, Davis used the GI Bill to attend Harvard to study under the noted international architect and Bauhaus founder, Walter Gropius. Due to the worsening political and social conditions in Germany, Gropius left his native country, first for England, then for America, where he accepted a position as a professor of architecture at Harvard in 1937. In 1938 he became director of the Department of Architecture at Harvard, a position he held until 1952. Gropius developed an influential program, attracting leading faculty members including Marcel Breuer, and many of the important new generation of American architects.[6]

Paul Rudolph, one of Gropius's most noted American students (as well as a classmate of Davis's at Harvard in 1946), attended Harvard before entering naval service in World War II. He returned after the war in 1946. Later he described his sense of honor at attending the school. "The Graduate School of Design is limited to fifteen and honestly I don't know exactly why I'm here among them." Continuing, he described Gropius's manner of working with graduate students. "The thing that I came for is so much more than I had thought it could possibly be . . . Mr. Gropius is the most dynamic man that I have ever come into contact with . . . He gives us individual instruction three times a week. Last Friday he had us out for cocktails at his famous home. There was a butler and his famous actress wife. She was truly charming and flirted with all of us."[7]

Gropius's "famous home" in Lincoln, Massachusetts, designed by Gropius and Marcel Breuer and completed in 1937, influenced Rudolph, Davis, and other students. It also served as a showcase for the international design influences espoused by Gropius and Breuer. Yet, as architectural historian Sigfried Giedion has observed, the house also incorporated conditions and materials used in America, with distinctive regional characteristics, offering lessons for students like Davis and Rudolph, who adapted them to their own environments. "This house is closely related, both in structure and composition, to all truly contemporary architecture: respect for the natural conditions of a particular region and the ability to fashion these to meet contemporary living requirements." Giedion concluded, naming this new direction: "This desire to create a harmonious relation between the present and the eternal—between the cosmos and the earthly environment—I have called the New Regionalism."[8]

Davis, like Rudolph, felt honored to study with Gropius and Breuer at Harvard and learned how the founder of the Bauhaus programs encouraged teamwork among students. His small graduate class, as Davis notes, included six American students and six foreign students, one of them, I. M. Pei. A faculty member, Hugh Stubbins, was later instrumental in Davis's acquisition of the teaching hospital commission in Berlin. Exposure to the faculty and students at Harvard established Davis's national path, one he extended when he accepted a position in the office of Eero Saarinen in Michigan. Saarinen, who was designing the noted General Motors Technical Center during Davis's time in the office, became famous for projects including the Jefferson National Expansion Memorial (the St. Louis Arch), the TWA Airlines Terminal at JFK International Airport, Dulles International Airport, the CBS Building in New York, and furniture forms, including his iconic Womb and Tulip chairs for Knoll.[9]

Then, apparently to his surprise, Davis agreed to return to New Orleans to create a new architectural firm, Curtis and Davis, accepting the invitation of his Tulane classmate, Nathaniel Curtis, whose father, Nathaniel Curtis Sr. was an influential professor of architecture at that school. He returned to his native region, bringing the lessons and professional associations he had established at Harvard and in Saarinen's office. From that foundation, he initiated the career that continues to the present date, one that had a profound influence upon the city and its architecture. And, despite saying that an architect "should not outlive his work," he has witnessed historic conditions impacting his work, and responds to the realities of this environment to protect his legacy.

The evolution of the Curtis and Davis firm reflected the growth of postwar New Orleans and the Gulf Coast South. In New Orleans, this included the expansion of the city into former marshlands and into growing suburbs such as Lakeview, Lake Vista, Gentilly, New Metaire, and eventually New Orleans East, after Interstate 10 was completed. The development of subdivisions and shopping centers, built along interstate highways and expanding road systems into once remote areas, drew residents from the city and older urban neighborhoods. After Katrina, many of these same low-lying neighborhoods were among those most devastated by flooding. They have remained the slowest to rebuild. Suburban neighborhoods included modern designs (including works by Curtis and Davis) in residences, schools, churches, and other structures that were severely damaged.[10]

Contemporary interest in the evolution of regional modern firms in locations across the country, from Florida to California, has contributed to a growing number of research projects, publications, and museum exhibitions in recent years. In California, for example, museum exhibitions and publications have reconsidered the importance of the Case Study House program, initiated in Los Angeles by *Arts and Architecture* magazine in 1945, as a way to encourage affordable alternatives in contemporary housing design during the postwar building boom. Widely reproduced Case Study Houses included CSH#8 (1945–49) by Charles and Ray Eames, CSH #20 (1947–48) by Richard Neutra, CSH #18, (1956–58) by Craig Ellwood, and perhaps most famously, CSH#22 (1959–1960) by Pierre Koenig, the well-known and often photographed Stahl House, built in the Hollywood Hills and cantilevered out over those hills and the surrounding environment.[11]

Other California modernists, including architects Richard Neutra, Harwell Hamilton Harris, and John Lautner, have generated growing recognition for their efforts to design structures in modern and traditional materials appropriate for the conditions and environments of their state.[12] Similarly, building upon the recognition given to the modern and contemporary architecture of Miami Beach, interest has focused on the evolution of modern architecture elsewhere in the state, especially in Sarasota. The recognition of a Sarasota School of Architecture, including architects as diverse as Ralph S. Twitchell, Paul Rudolph, Ralph and William Zimmerman, Gene Leedy, and others, has been a significant development in the past decade. Additionally, growing recognition comes increasingly to the architecture of Paul Rudolph, including his residential and public projects in Florida.[13]

In New Orleans and along the Gulf Coast, Curtis and Davis reflected an awareness of these national and regional trends, evident in their efforts to bring modern styles and influences into harmony with regional materials, vernacular traditions, environmental considerations, and social customs. They focused on a wide range of projects and building types including private and public housing, schools and universities, churches and religious structures, governmental buildings, hospitals and medical facilities, prisons and correctional institutions as well as commercial and industrial projects.

In his text, Davis refers to an important early commission for his friend Edgar B. Stern, Jr., who lived on Garden Lane and wanted a new swimming pool. As the scope of the pool project evolved to include a form that incorporated more of the property, Stern's mother, Edith Stern, became involved in the conversation. Mrs. Stern, whose own nearby home, LongVue, is now a museum and garden property, was part of the Sears-Roebuck family and a major philanthropist who supported social, educational, and arts projects. Her approval of the pool was not inconsequential for the young architect. Soon after, he was commissioned by Edgar Stern to design a new hotel project in the French Quarter, the Royal Orleans, which became the first in a series of hotel projects for this client.

Other residential commissions came from clients including Dr. Morris Sushan and Mr. and Mrs. William Christovich. An early residential project, a house for Walter B. Moses, Jr., located on Audubon Boulevard, offered Davis the opportunity to apply the lessons learned from the Gropius home to an uptown home in New Orleans (which came to include an original sculpture designed for the house by Alexander Calder). Typical of these projects was an interest in modern architecture enhanced by their clients' love of the natural environment of their properties, with some located in traditional neighborhoods, others in developing suburban and lakefront areas, often featuring historic trees that were integrated into the design by the young architects.

The designing of contemporary houses for clients with traditional tastes, often on properties in historic neighborhoods, offered challenges and opportunities for the young firm. One example is the house designed for Mr. and Mrs. Julian Steinberg in the Garden District of New Orleans, one of the city's most historic areas. The property was once part of the large James Robb estate just off Washington Avenue, which was for a time an early home of Newcomb College. Their client preferred, as Davis notes, a Palm Beach style cottage. The architects dissuaded him of this interest and created one of their most significant contemporary residences, now undergoing an extensive restoration for the current owners, John and Lynn Fishback, under the direction of New Orleans architect Lee Ledbetter.

And in addition to client homes, Arthur Davis created important houses for his own family, including an early one near Lake Pontchartrain, in the Lake Vista area. Then he found a property near the Edgar Stern house, on Bamboo Road, and built a house that used the same lift-slab construction process he and Curtis had used in the construction of Angola Prison. Later he included a separate studio and guest house, reminiscent of the additions completed by Phillip Johnson on his noted Glass House property in Connecticut (now a museum complex and part of the National Historic Trust). Arthur and Mary Davis welcomed important guests to this house.

After he inherited a historic house in the French Quarter from a colleague, Davis moved again, enlarging the home by incorporating a contemporary wing that reflected the materials, styles, and traditions of the French Quarter. No doubt, his Tulane training and assignments in the French Quarter added to his understanding of the architecture of the district and to the challenge of adding contemporary components to this property. Most recently, he converted a warehouse near the Convention Center, in the Warehouse Arts District, into a large loft home and office space, where he continues to live and work today.

Public housing became an important architectural tradition in New Orleans, beginning in the Roosevelt era of the 1930s, and offered opportunities for new architectural programs after World War II. During the Depression era, public housing was built in neighborhoods across the city—offering important prototypes for a range of prewar approaches to humane public housing. In New Orleans a smaller, brick courtyard-style garden form evolved as a standard housing type—standing a few stories tall, with a limited number of units per structure—the model was residential, with cast iron ornamentation, ceramic roof tiles, and references to the historic architecture of New Orleans. Commonly, these were situated among native trees and built around grass playgrounds, with front-yard-like environments. These housing projects established new prototypes, especially when maintenance and security standards were enforced. In later decades, when security, maintenance, and social conditions deteriorated, these once-admired complexes became centers for crime and gang wars, bringing a major shift in public perception.

After the war, Curtis and Davis explored the modern option of taller public housing units, moving beyond the older style in New Orleans, reflecting broader national directions, and causing controversy with local architects and public housing officials. They argued that vertical building made more sense, allowing more available land mass to be dedicated to collective parks, playgrounds, and resident use. Guste Homes became a model for the type of experimentation they advocated, yet initially only skeptical response greeted them. Over time, however, their model was proven to be successful and did not fall into the decline evident with projects in cities such as New York, Chicago, and St. Louis, many of them now destroyed. Their housing project still functions, in post-Katrina New Orleans.

In post-Katrina New Orleans, public housing projects became battlegrounds, pitting those who wanted them destroyed and rebuilt as new housing types against those who wanted them reopened and put into use for returning citizens and workers. These controversies were covered regularly in the national media. In response, the Ogden Museum organized an exhibition of housing project photographs by *New York Times* photographer, Fred Conrad, which were featured in a *New York Times* article written by architectural critic, Nicolai Orrouseff. Despite protests, lawsuits, and national media coverage, by the summer of 2008 almost all of these housing projects were demolished. Only the Curtis and Davis project in Central City remains in relatively original condition, with a significant occupancy rate. For Davis, as indicated in his text, this stands as a victory for a once-controversial design (one criticized as well by members of the local chapter of the AIA.)

An important part of Davis's career and his relationship to the evolving social and racial history of New Orleans is related to the design of schools in the postwar era. His architecture developed during a period of radical social and cultural change—reflecting both the optimism of postwar Eisenhower America and, in contrast, the continuing and contradictory realities of a segregated South (and nation). Black and white students did not attend the same public schools, sit at the same lunch counters, or ride in the same sections of public streetcars in New Orleans. Public schools and state universities became battlegrounds for the civil rights efforts of the 1950s, beginning with the *Brown v. Board of Education* Supreme Court decision of 1954, and leading to President Eisenhower's order to send federal troops to integrate Little Rock High School in the fall of 1957.

Quietly, in their determined and focused way, Curtis and Davis designed schools that brought the promise of a new South and an equal educational experience to all social and racial levels of New Orleans, including the majority black student population. Thomy Lafon School became a national model of this enlightened direction, as both a social experiment and as a source of architectural innovation for national and regional schools. The school was well documented in the major architectural journals and also in the most popular national magazine of the period, *Life* magazine.

Built next to one of the city's oldest and largest public housing projects, also recently demolished, Thomy Lafon offered additional challenges, primarily in the need to retain a number of the older school's buildings for use, requiring that Curtis and Davis create a plan that used only a portion of the total property. Their solution earned them national recognition and awards. They elevated the structure, as Davis explains in his text, creating a series of protected spaces for children and playground activities, raising the classrooms above street level, incorporating open breezes and cooling winds in an era before air conditioning was common in Southern schools. And, as local observers noted, even in their modern design, they paid homage to raised vernacular architectural forms evident across New Orleans and the state of Louisiana, reflecting their regional roots.

National architectural journals praised the school and the architectural program for this challenging project, bringing professional recognition to the young New Orleans firm and showcasing their ability to apply modern design principles to social and racial conditions in the South. Equally impressed, the writers of *Life* magazine showed students happily engaged with the school and its playgrounds, images of a 1950s that defied the stereotypes portrayed in the national media, especially in depictions of public education for blacks in the South. Children in uniforms crossed the campus and ramps of Lafon, passed art that was incorporated into the project, and looked through windows toward a future that seemed years ahead of the year, 1953.

A similarly progressive campus and school plan was developed for a large project near the Ninth Ward of the city, the Carver High School and Junior High School project, to be built adjoining an elementary school, as part of a new campus planning approach to public schools in the city. Carver, built around a campus plan of major consequence, also incorporated innovative engineering and construction systems.

In addition to public schools, Curtis and Davis acquired commissions for a series of Catholic churches and schools in New Orleans and elsewhere in the state. Their first church was completed on the city's West Bank in Marrero (then only recently connected to downtown New Orleans by a massive new bridge across the Mississippi River), a small structure for the Church of the Immaculate Conception. A larger and more open plan was completed for Our Lady Queen of Heaven Church in Lake Charles, an elegant modernist church that has survived a variety of storms (including Hurricane Rita) in that part of the state, and continues to function and support its parish.

The largest and most prominent of their churches was St. Francis Cabrini Church, located on Paris Avenue in the Gentilly neighborhood of New Orleans (one of most damaged areas following Hurricane Katrina). Originally, this neighborhood's growth reflected the suburban evolution of the city toward Lake Pontchartrain and the University of New Orleans's lakefront campus, an important direction for growing middle-class families in New Orleans. The church was designed for a large congregation, with an open-aisle seating plan for eight hundred parishioners. The central altar was topped by a soaring sixty-foot spire, capped by a dome, gold-leafed on its underside, designed to float over the altar. During a period of postwar development and expansion in the Catholic Church, in one of the nation's most Catholic cities, this became a high profile and highly valued project. The church was covered by a floating concrete shell structure, similar to the one constructed for the Rivergate in downtown New Orleans.

Public buildings by Curtis and Davis appeared in the commercial center of the city as well as in developing suburban neighborhoods. One of the most prominent structures was the New Orleans Public Library, built as part of the Civic Plaza associated with a new City Hall complex, which included the City Hall building and related legal and judicial structures. The library was planned and built under the direction of a progressive new leader who requested a "department store" approach, with a modern and highly inviting public library intentionally created in contrast to older library structures, which were reflective of Beaux Arts design and operational principles. At the time of its completion, public libraries, like public schools, served as centers for education, and a progressive public library was an important symbol, especially in the Deep South.

In New Orleans, during the 1950s and 1960s, a progressive business and political vision emerged in New Orleans, seeking to place the old port city into more direct competition with Southern cites including Atlanta, Dallas, and Houston. As expressways were built and transportation modes shifted toward the automobile, the city was reformed, though not always for the better, with many historic structures demolished, including train stations designed by Louis Sullivan and Burnham and Root, as well as landmarks in the history of jazz—all lost to "urban renewal."[14] However, the growth of the city and the expansion of local companies created new clients for the Curtis and Davis firm, resulting in projects including the Caribe Building, the Automotive Life Building, the Pan American Life Insurance Company, the Louisiana Power & Light Building, the Luzianne Coffee Plant, and the Oakwood Shopping Center. The firm increasingly became involved in regional and national office building design, creating, for example, structures for IBM in cities including Nashville, Jackson, Shreveport, Mobile, and Pittsburgh.

A different type of public structure evolved when Curtis and Davis received the commission to design a progressive prison for the State of Louisiana at Angola, a notoriously ominous environment. Using the lift-slab engineering and construction technique, along with a more open and modern design—incorporating natural light and views, in stark contrast to the older prison design—they created a model institution, in the place of one considered to be one of the worst in the nation. In turn, this project supplied engineering and construction techniques they used in other projects, as well as the lift slab technique used in the construction of Davis's new house. And, from this project, they received a number of other national prison and correctional institution projects.

Hotels grew into a major focus of the firm, beginning in New Orleans. From the relationship with Edgar Stern, Jr., and Davis's pool design for his Garden Lane home, two projects in New Orleans evolved, the Royal Orleans and Royal Sonesta Hotels in the French Quarter. Both faced challenges as new hotels because they were to be built in a protected, historic part of the city. The Royal Orleans was built on the site of one of the city's most historic hotels, the St. Louis Hotel, once a center for the city's Creole society, which was destroyed in a 1915 hurricane. The hotel reflected the city's complex history, from its high style social life to the infamy of the city's standing as a major slave market, with part of the hotel used as a prominent slave auction site. The design for the new hotel reflected an awareness of this history and integrated architectural elements of the original structure into its design. It was so well received that an addition was completed in 1963.

The success and planning evident in the New Orleans hotel projects led to significant new hotel commissions in a variety of locations, including several through Davis's ties to the Stern family. One of these was the Stanford Court Hotel in San Francisco, which was followed by two large projects, a condominium village in Park City, Utah, and a new community in Huntington Beach, California. Through the Stern association, and the success of the Royal Sonesta Hotel, owned by the Sonnabend group, Curtis and Davis began to work directly with Sonnabend on a series of hotels including the renovation of the Plaza Hotel in New York, and a series of hotels in Europe. By the end of the 1950s, Curtis and Davis had opened an office in New York and one in London. The London office was located in the Carlton Hotel, part of the Hotel Corporation of America, tied to Roger Sonnabend. They completed a renovation to the Carlton Tower, built a new hotel at Heathrow Airport, designed a new hotel for the historic St. Andrews golf course in Scotland, and also completed hotel designs in Detroit, Michigan; Hartford, Connecticut; and Cambridge, Massachusetts.

New Orleans became a growing medical and medical university center, and the Curtis and Davis firm became connected to the health provider community and its need for expanded facilities and office buildings, creating projects for Oschner Hospital, Touro Infirmary, and others. They also created a series of small clinics across the state, including the Sako Clinic in Raceland, a simple, elevated structure designed to reflect both modern medical needs and the Japanese heritage and sensibilities of their client. This structure was the first to incorporate their use of masonry and tile screen elements, a device later applied to their design for the

American Embassy in Saigon, Vietnam. That embassy, which reflects their architectural experiences on the Gulf Coast, was featured in some of the most reproduced photographs from the war in Vietnam, many focused on the evacuation of the embassy. It is one of the firm's most recognized international projects, yet few people could name the architects who designed it.

Their experiences with medical facilities in Louisiana, and the architectural and political associations of the firm, led to their acquisition of one of the period's most important medical commissions, a new teaching hospital in Berlin. This became a major focus for Arthur Davis, from the late 1950s well into the 1960s. He witnessed political and social changes on a profound level, as he describes in his text, ranging from the coming of John F. Kennedy to Berlin, to the construction of the Berlin Wall and the hardening of attitudes between East and West Germany, accompanied by related acts on his part including the transporting of people across the borders in his old Mercedes. More importantly, Davis planned and oversaw the construction of a massive teaching hospital, combining the teaching philosophies and practices of East and West. It remains one of his proudest achievements as an architect and to some degree as a diplomat involved in the range of international political activities required to complete such a challenging project.

Planning and architectural practices by Curtis and Davis came to include colleges and universities in New Orleans, including Tulane University and LSU at New Orleans, now the University of New Orleans. At Tulane, they designed buildings such as the Tulane University Center (sensitively expanded and renovated recently) and a major science building. The planning and building of a major urban university campus on the New Orleans lakefront, on a site occupied by an airfield during the war, reflected the maturing of the city as well as its place in the postwar economic and educational boom. With the GI Bill and related incentives to advance to new levels in education and employment attracting a growing number of Americans, new urban university programs were a central part of this development, especially for first generation college students.

Unique in the South and in the state of Louisiana, LSU at New Orleans, under founding Chancellor Homer Hitt, opened in 1958 as an integrated campus, quite in contrast to the protests, violence, use of federal troops, and acts of confrontation by public and elected officials evident at campuses such as the University of Mississippi, the University of Alabama, the University of Georgia, and others across the South. The campus opened in 1958 with a campus plan and core number of structures by Curtis and Davis, including the Liberal Arts Building. The campus plan, acknowledging its history as a military base, incorporated the use of those older military structures and initially parts of the airstrip were allowed to remain evident. In 2008, UNO launched a series of celebrations marking its fiftieth anniversary, including an exploration of its architectural history, a process Arthur Davis has witnessed evolving from its inception.

Beginning in the late 1960s, and continuing into the 1970s and 1980s, metropolitan New Orleans evolved, consciously building upon its past and its unique culture and heritage, reflected in the growing appeal of the French Quarter for tourists, while looking to a more diverse contemporary future through new economic endeavors—building upon prospects for the oil business, trade, and the Mississippi River port, as well as new directions in the convention and tourism industry—all creating opportunities for Davis and his partners. Davis spent his childhood in a city that was rooted in the nineteenth century. In the later decades of the twentieth century, he was able to build upon that history and his

understanding of it, to became an active participant in the planning and building of a more modern vision of the city, interweaving it into the historical fabric of New Orleans.

Writing in his 1982 book, *A Short History of New Orleans*, Mel Leavitt offered a vision of the city at that moment in history, observing that New Orleans had "managed to conquer the swamp, control and direct the river, and build a towering metropolis on one side of Canal Street while preserving the historic ambiance of its venerable Vieux Carre." Leavitt pointed to successes in tourism, the oil economy, trade, and the expansion of the port with its planned "ultramodern" Centroport complex, and referred to the evolution of the Poydras Street corridor, noting that "1980 saw eight new office buildings either completed or under construction, averaging 27 stories in height, [with] a total investment of $193 million." And he called the growth of tourism "astounding," explaining that the city "played host to over six million visitors in 1980. More than 800 conventions were held in New Orleans. Ten years ago, there were fewer than 4,000 first-class hotel rooms downtown. Now there are more than 20,000; many more are planned."[15]

At the time Leavitt's book was released, the city was advancing its planning for a World's Fair to be presented downtown (1984–85), along the riverfront and the edge of the area now known as the Warehouse Arts District. Davis supported this vision for the city, indicated by the locating of his architectural office and residence, where he still lives, only blocks from the fair site. Increasingly, from the 1970s to the present, the growth of New Orleans and the Gulf South region has reflected the larger evolution of the American South. Massive new populations have moved to the South and the "Sunbelt," as have national and international businesses, corporations, and research centers—automotive manufacturing and high tech companies have built plants in once remote agricultural regions, aerospace companies have developed facilities, airport and warehousing operations have grown, and medical research centers have expanded.

Arthur Davis realized that new opportunities were developing in this larger environment and his architectural and planning vision expanded as he worked during the past three decades in the Curtis and Davis, DMJM Curtis and Davis, and Arthur Q. Davis FAIA and Partners firms. Davis and his partners were involved in the design and building of four of New Orleans's most prominent public structures of this era—all oriented toward national and regional events including conventions, major league and college sports, concerts, trade shows, and related activities (including Mardi Gras events)—the Rivergate, the Louisiana Superdome, UNO's Keifer Lakefront Arena, and the New Orleans Arena. With the growth of these facilities and the expansion of the convention center, more hotels were needed. Davis and his partners designed large new hotel projects including the Marriott Hotel on Canal Street and the Hyatt Hotel adjoining the Superdome. Through DMJM Curtis and Davis, he participated in the construction of the second downtown bridge across the Mississippi River—the Crescent City Connection, linking the city's east and west banks. And, during the last decade, as the convention and tourism industries expanded in New Orleans, Davis remained active in diverse ways, including his role in the opening and planned expansion of the National D-Day Museum (now the National World War II Museum) in the Warehouse Arts District.

One of the Curtis and Davis firm's major civic projects was the Rivergate (1968–1995), a convention and exhibition facility constructed of reinforced concrete, marked by a flowing barrel-arched roof design (reflecting the Mississippi River), that was considered a major architectural and engineering landmark in the city. Built at the intersection of Canal and Poydras Streets, across from the new World Trade Center (designed by Edward Durrell Stone) near the Mississippi River, it marked a symbolic shift away from the river and the port's earlier incarnations, as docking and warehousing activities were being relocated upriver (during the transition to container shipping), toward a more public usage. The Rivergate, reflecting the city's increasing focus on attracting conventions and national tourism, also became a popular local center for special events and civic activities, including Mardi Gras balls and high school graduations. Though the Rivergate was a signature building for Curtis and Davis and a civic landmark for the architecture and engineering community, it was threatened and ultimately destroyed to make way for a new casino project (now the site of Harrah's Casino), an event that was a turning point for the architectural and preservation communities of the city.[16]

And, for Arthur Davis and his partner Buster Curtis, this was a critical lesson about the vulnerability of their projects, even prominent civic buildings, and the appreciation of modern architecture in the city and its preservation communities. For Davis, even in 2008, it remains a bitter lesson, one he addressed in writing not long after the destruction of the Rivergate. "There is no question . . . that the Rivergate was a significant monument in the city of New Orleans. It would have been a significant building in any city in the world. It was an expression of the sixties . . . Intended to be an exhibition hall, the Rivergate was a graceful and romantic structure using reinforced concrete in a way that was light and delicate." He noted that whether "a building is thirty years old or a hundred and thirty years old should have no significance at all whether the building should be recognized as important. If a building is important, it should be recognized and protected. It is as simple as that!" Concluding, he offered the following sentiments. "The Rivergate could easily have been converted to a casino . . . But politicians made the decision to squander the building and squander the money to tear it down. There was great opportunity for New Orleans . . . The opportunity has been lost forever."[17]

The most famous building by the Curtis and Davis firm, and certainly one of the most recognized buildings in the world, the Louisiana Superdome, became a symbol of New Orleans even before it opened in 1975. From its earliest announcement, reporting on the Superdome was marked by the use of massive quantifying numbers, as indicated in an article published in the August 25, 1975, issue of *Time*. "This week, a decade after Houston opened its Astrodome and pronounced it the Eighth Wonder of the World, New Orleans will stage the 'grand opening' of its 97,365 capacity Louisiana Superdome, which could absorb the 66,000 seat Astrodome with room to spare." Describing the "27-story-high Superdome, which resembles a giant flying saucer set down on 52 acres of downtown New Orleans," and its cost which "ballooned from $35 million to $163 million," as "the largest room ever built for human use," *Time* continued, offering an expanding list of facts. "The windowless building, sheathed in gold, anodized aluminum, boasts over 75,000 sq. yds. of carpeting and contains 9,000 tons of computerized air conditioning and heating equipment; its energy costs are estimated at $1,752,000 a year." In this article, then Governor Edwin Edwards, an individual seldom recognized for a sense of understatement, described it as "the greatest structure of its kind ever envisioned by mankind."[18]

Describing the Superdome in his 1996 monograph on the building, Marty Mule writes of its larger symbolism for the city: "The futuristic contours of the Superdome, and its glistening roof, in two decades have become as much symbols of the Crescent City as the two-century-old façade of St. Louis Cathedral, or Jackson Square."[19] New Orleans sports

writer Peter Finney observed that it is where "Pope John Paul II prayed, also a building where Michael Jordan threw up a prayer . . . It's a building where Mick Jagger and George Bush drew standing ovations, also a building where the same thing happened for Joe Montana and Muhammad Ali."[20] The Superdome, located near the French Quarter, the Central Business District, and downtown hotels, established the stature of New Orleans as a "major league city," as a center for professional sports—including Super Bowls, Final Fours, the Sugar Bowl, and countless NCAA and NFL games—along with events like the Republican National Convention and concerts by performers including the Rolling Stones, Frank Sinatra, Willie Nelson, and Bette Midler. For decades after its opening, the Superdome served as a successful symbol of New Orleans, even as other domed arenas became obsolete. Then, at least initially, Hurricane Katrina seemed to end that.

For Arthur Davis, a most memorable event was the Superdome's recovery from the damage inflicted upon it during Hurricane Katrina—the extensive physical damage and the damage to its reputation—after it became a symbol for a crisis in government and leadership, reflected in the abandonment of the city's poorest citizens in a storm-damaged structure, all broadcast on national television. *Time* noted that the "National Guard reported six deaths in the Superdome, four by natural causes, one by drug overdose, and one by apparent suicide. Four other bodies were found in the street outside the Dome." Many reported that the Superdome would remain closed, then demolished, following Katrina. Yet, less than a year later, and much to Arthur Davis's joy, the Superdome was repaired and preparing for its grand reopening, focused on a football game between the New Orleans Saints and the Atlanta Falcons, on September 25, 2006, as reported in *Time*. "The Superdome now smells of paint. A $185 million construction project continues, and stainless steel countertops illuminate the concession stands. The largest roofing job in American history is complete. Paul Tagliabue, the retiring NFL commissioner, said he would start an exhibit at the Pro Football Hall of Fame to honor the new Superdome."[21]

After the Superdome, the Curtis and Davis firm had obtained another major state project when they were awarded the design for a new lakefront sports facility and performance venue for the East Campus of the University of New Orleans (later named the Nat Kiefer Lakefront Arena). Designed to serve as a home for the UNO basketball team and other sports events, it became a successful mid-sized venue for concerts and performing arts programs. In 1987, during his visit to New Orleans, Pope Paul II performed an open-air mass on the grounds of the Lakefront Arena to a reported audience of over 100,000 people. Then, in 2005, the Lakefront Arena, like the Superdome, was heavily damaged by Hurricane Katrina and its aftermath; however, it remained closed for a longer period. Finally, on May 2, 2008, following an extensive program of repair and renovation costing $25 million, the arena reopened and returned to its role in the public life of the university and the community. Again, this was most welcome news for Arthur Davis.

In the 1990s, Davis had obtained a commission from the state for a third arena in New Orleans, this time through his later firm, Arthur Q. Davis FAIA and Partners, for the New Orleans Arena, located downtown next to the Superdome. Working in association with Billes-Manning Architects and Hewitt-Washington and Associates, Davis designed the New Orleans Arena to be connected to the existing HVAC and mechanical systems of the Superdome as well as its parking garages, offering an efficient and practical solution for a needed smaller venue for performances and civic events, as well as a potential venue for a future basketball team. The Arena opened to the public on October 29, 1999. Not long after the

building opened, it accomplished one of its major missions when the Charlotte Hornets relocated to New Orleans. This structure reinforced the city's ability to attract conventions and other national events that supported the downtown, French Quarter, and regional economy, reflecting once again, Davis's role in the evolution of the city of New Orleans over the past sixty years.

Another, more recent project in New Orleans that has remained important to Davis was the planning and opening of the National D-Day Museum in the Warehouse Arts District, guided by the vision of Dr. Stephen Ambrose, a noted author and professor of history of the University of New Orleans. Davis has remained active with the board of the museum as it evolved into the National World War II Museum and participated in planning activities related to the architectural selection process and development of a long-term program for the museum's extensive expansion program (now in process). His own naval experiences in World War II also made him a member of the veterans' groups who have embraced the museum and also offered a forum for his expanded research and discussion of his own war efforts, especially in the area of painting and camouflage techniques and their application to ships in the Pacific theater.

And, while it is not directly related to his role in the developing history of architecture in New Orleans, Davis's work in designing a master plan for Kuala Kencana, a new town in Indonesia, is related to his association with local corporate and business leaders, including the leaders of Freeport Mc-MoRan, with offices in New Orleans, whose business interests in mining copper and gold brought this project into the early stages of its evolution. From the beginning of his professional career, Davis and his diverse partners were active in large scale planning and related architectural design programs. The Kuala Kencana project was a logical outgrowth of those earlier activities and allowed Davis to apply his regional studies and design experiences to another unique region with its own set of geographical and climate conditions.

During the summer of 2005, when Davis was eighty-five years old and still working with his partners in the restored warehouse building on Julia Street, located directly across from Emeril's Restaurant, he might have assumed that his architectural legacy was well established and secure. The architectural symbols of his diverse firms' accomplishments surrounded him downtown, including the Superdome, the New Orleans Arena, the Marriott and Hyatt hotels, and the Crescent City Connection. Davis also might have assumed that his remaining projects and consulting programs would follow a normally predictable path, winding down his long career in a logical fashion, allowing him time for reflection, travel, and the enjoyment of the well-known social and cultural amenities of the city. That all changed on August 29, 2005.

Like so many residents of New Orleans, Davis and his wife Mary evacuated the city, assuming their departure would last for only a few days until the storm passed. They traveled first to rural Mississippi, staying at the country home of Dr. Sidhartha Bhansali, whose residence was designed by Davis. Then the Davises traveled to Jackson, Mississippi, and on to Houston. After a short stay there, they moved to Dallas, and later back to Houston, before finally returning to New Orleans after an extended evacuation. While the city had suffered extensive damage, downtown and the Warehouse Arts District areas survived. Arthur and Mary Davis returned to find their home in livable condition with minimal damage. In that, they were more fortunate than many who returned. Yet, as Davis soon realized, the impact of the storm and the

related flooding upon his city, and the many projects associated with his career, was a very different matter.

During his childhood, Davis and his family had witnessed the destructive power of nature during the great Mississippi flood of 1927. Now, during the eighty-fifth year of his life, in the first decade of the twenty-first century, he witnessed a new paradigm of natural and manmade destruction in New Orleans and along the Gulf Coast region. Hurricane Katrina made landfall on the Gulf Coast on August 29, 2005, and within twenty-four hours the extensive levee and canal system of New Orleans began to fail. The 17th Street Canal, the London Avenue Canal, and the Industrial Canal failed, and water poured into the city, stranding those who had remained behind. Rescue efforts in the Superdome, the Convention Center, and across the city were woefully inadequate and prolonged, bringing national and international scrutiny in the wake of the storm. And, along with the rest of the city, a number of the projects designed by Davis and his partners suffered extensive water damage.

After returning and connecting to the initial recovery programs of the city, Davis became involved in the process of planning the city's return. His years of experience and his larger understanding of the history and evolution of the city and its neighborhood development patterns proved to be valuable assets. On a more direct level, he tracked the status of his early and more recent projects, monitoring their conditions and their levels of survivability. He worked as a consultant to owners of some projects, reviewing plans and providing valuable historical insight into the evolution and design of diverse residential, commercial, and institutional projects.

Like so many other residents of New Orleans, he did what he could to assist the slow recovery efforts in the city he had known since childhood. As national and international architects, designers, preservation experts, and urban planners increasingly arrived in the city, assessing the damage and beginning the process of planning for the future, attention began to focus slowly on the status and legacy of the city's twentieth-century architecture, including many of the projects associated with Davis's career. The works of the Curtis and Davis firm were featured prominently in the "Regional Modernism" exhibition presented at the Ogden Museum in the summer of 2007, bringing renewed attention to Davis and his progressive vision.

Writing about the exhibition for the *Times-Picayune* in July 2007, in an article titled "Modern Dilemma: The Struggle between Honoring Historical Buildings and Embracing the City's Future," art critic Doug MacCash noted that the city still struggled to accept architectural styles designed by Davis and other modernists decades earlier. Reviewing the exhibition and an accompanying video, MacCash focused upon the importance of Arthur Davis. "The embattled hero of the video, the exhibit, and the whole modernist period is architect Arthur Q. Davis, who, as part of the Curtis and Davis firm, gave New Orleans several of its most revolutionary modern structures, such as the undulating Rivergate Convention Center (1968), the supersonic-gothic Automotive Life Insurance building (1963), and the diamond-edged New Orleans Arena (1999)." Continuing, he notes that despite their "relative youth, some of Davis's structures already have fallen into disrepair and others have been demolished. In the video, the aging but authoritative Davis poignantly says: 'I'd hate to think it's a trend that I'm outliving my buildings.'"[22]

In 2007 and 2008, as a growing number of architectural advocates and architectural preservationists work to save endangered landmarks of the modernist era in New Orleans, including those associated with Davis and his career, he continues to do what he can to insure the survival of that legacy. In addition to his consulting activities, during this time he has worked consistently on the manuscript of his personal and professional memoirs for publication in a future book. This is that book.

Notes

1.   Sherwood Anderson, "New Orleans, the *Double Dealer* and the Modern Movement in America," in Judy Long, ed., *Literary New Orleans* (Athens: Hill Street Press, 1999), 85–86.

2.   See John Barry, *Rising Tide: The Great Mississippi Flood of 1927 and How It Changed America* (New York: Simon & Schuster, 1997).

3.   See Robert D. Leighninger Jr., *Building Louisiana: The Legacy of the Public Works Administration* (Jackson: University Press of Mississippi, 2007).

4.   Federal Writers' Project of the Works Progress Administration for the City of New Orleans, *New Orleans City Guide* (Boston: Houghton Mifflin Company, 1938), 145, 155.

5.   Ibid, 82.

6.   See Gilbert Lupfer and Paul Sigel, *Walter Gropius, 1883–1969: The Promoter of a New Form* (Koln: Tashen, 2004); Hans Engels and Ulf Meyer, *Bauhaus: 1919–1933* (Munchen: Presetel, 2006); and Robert F. Gatje, *Marcel Breuer: A Memoir* (New York: The Monacelli Press, 2000).

7.   Christopher Domin and Joseph King, *Paul Rudolph: The Florida Houses* (New York: Princeton Architectural Press, 2002), 28.

8.   Ibid, 30.

9.   See Pierluigi Serraino, *Eero Saarinen, 1910–1961* (Koln: Taschen, 2005).

10. See Mary Lou Widmer, *New Orleans in the Fifties* (Gretna: Pelican Publishing Company, 2004), 55–69, 107–19.

11. See Elizabeth A. T. Smith, *Case Study Houses, 1945–1966: The California Impetus* (Koln: Taschen, 2006) and James Steele and David Jenkins, *Pierre Koenig* (London: Phaidon, 1998).

12. See Barbara Lamprecht, *Richard Neutra, 1892–1970: Survival through Design* (Koln: Taschen, 2004); Lisa Germany, *Harwell Hamilton Harris* (Berkeley: University of California Press, 2000); and Barbara-Ann Campbell-Lange, *John Lautner, 1911–1994: Disappearing Space* (Koln: Taschen, 2005). And for a recent museum examination of the culture of the state and its relationship to art and design at mid-century, see Elizabeth Armstrong, *Birth of the Cool: California Art, Design, and Culture at Midcentury* (Newport Beach: Orange County Museum of Art and Pestel Publishing, 2007).

13. See John Howey, *The Sarasota School of Architecture, 1941–1966* (Cambridge: The MIT Press, 1997); Domin and King, *Paul Rudolph: The Florida Houses*; and Jan Hochstim, *Florida Modern: Residential Architecture, 1945–1970* (New York: Rizzoli, 2004).

14. For a more extensive consideration of these issues, see J. Richard Gruber, Jim Rapier, and Mary Beth Romig, *Phillip Collier's Missing New Orleans* (New Orleans: The Ogden Museum of Southern Art, 2005).

15. Mel Leavitt, *A Short History of New Orleans* (San Francisco: LEXIKOS, 1982), 152–53.

16. For a consideration of the Rivergate and the preservation controversies associated with its demolition, see *The Rivergate (1968–1995), Architecture and Politics, No Strangers in Pair-A-Dice, A 20th Century Masterpiece Destroyed by Louisiana's Gambling Blitz* (New Orleans: Tulane Howard-Tilton Memorial Library, 2000), also available as an on-line document (www.tulane.edu/-rivgate).

17. Ibid, Chapter 11.

18. "The Biggest Dome," *Time*, August 25, 1975.

19. Marty Mule, *Superdome: Thirteen Acres That Changed New Orleans* (Mandeville: Gulf South Books, 1996), 17–18.

20. Ibid.

21. "Superdome Stars: Everyday People Confronted Chaos," *Time*, August 6, 2006.

22. Doug MacCash, "Modern Dilemma: The Struggle between Honoring Historical Buildings and Embracing the City's Future Continues at the Ogden," *Times-Picayune*, July 20, 2007.

It Happened by Design

Arthur Davis, c. 1921.

It Happened by Design

In the late nineteenth and early twentieth centuries, my family was in the rice planting and milling business in the town of Point-a-La-Hache, Louisiana, south of New Orleans on the Mississippi River delta. Through the years, floods destroyed our lands. Some flooding was caused by nature, but the flood of 1927 was caused by man. The land was inundated unnecessarily, allegedly with the intent of protecting the city of New Orleans. The Levee Board took the land away from us, saying it was needed to build and maintain levees. Three decades later, the Legislature returned our land to my family, though we are still engaged in a legal battle to determine how much of the revenue from the oil and gas under the land belongs to us and how much belongs to the Levee Board.

Before I was born on March 30, 1920, my parents and other members of my family moved to New Orleans, and from time to time we have gone down to Point-a-la-Hache to visit. When I was a little boy, my uncle David Davis used to take me fishing around Point-a-la-Hache and Shell Beach. We caught tremendous amounts of fish. The area is still very raw but has a primitive beauty. A number of people still living down there knew our family from generations back, and on one occasion we were tramping through the swamps around some of the nineteenth-century homes, not mansions but quite palatial in their own right. As I approached a cottage, there was a call from the front porch. "Come on up here and let me visit with you. I know who you are. I can tell by the way you walk. You have the Davis walk, which is unique and can be recognized anywhere." This was the voice of Dr. Bellou. He was at one time the general practitioner for that part of the parish. He had long retired and lived in a cottage on the Haspel-Davis property. We sat and visited for quite some time, and he regaled me with many stories of my parents, grandparents, and great-grandparents, and perhaps even three or four generations before, who all lived on the land and worked not only at

rice planting but also at the rice mills. The old gentleman was very complimentary as far as the Davis family was concerned, and I appreciated hearing from himçç that we survived an honorable lifestyle up until the time the failure of the levees destroyed our property. He also told of the family ghosts of Point-a-la-Hache who walked the Haspel-Davis plantation.

We were not economically deprived, and I was given the benefit of a good education at one of the best private schools in New Orleans. My early education was uneventful. I was an average student with the exceptions of a course in freehand drawing and one in drafting. In these two subjects I excelled, but in all other areas I had little motivation to do more than was necessary to get by. I was involved in athletics—basketball, football, and running hurdles.

The entire direction of my life was changed in a few moments—during one innocuous event. At the age of fourteen, while riding a bicycle through Audubon Park, I noticed an old brick mason building a fireplace on a lot on Walnut Street facing the park. The mason was laying the brick in a herringbone pattern indicated on a blueprint that he had tacked to a plywood board. I was fascinated by his dexterity and the beauty with which he handled the trowel, how he set each brick in this very intricate pattern with such ease. I parked my bike and sat on the curb watching him for quite some time until I finally mustered the courage to ask how he decided on the beautiful designs he was creating on the brick chimney.

He said, "I use this blueprint which tells me exactly how many courses, where to project the bricks, and where to recess the bricks. This information is given to me on the print which was prepared by the architect for this house we are building on this site."

I had never seen a blueprint, and I was astounded to see the white lines on blue paper with dimensions and rather interesting diagrams describing exactly how the chimney

Above: Arthur Davis, c. 1925.

Left: Arthur Davis's maternal grandparents and family.

should be built and how it was to become an integral part of the house. This impressed me tremendously and from that moment forward I knew I wanted to be able to produce the drawings that would permit these talented craftsmen to build buildings. It was as simple as that. There was never any doubt in my mind that I was going to be an architect.

While still a high school student, since I was convinced that I would become an architect and had two years of mechanical drawing, I was able to obtain summer employment as an apprentice for five dollars a week with Weiss, Dreyfess, & Seifert, the major architectural firm in the state at that time. It was designing the Louisiana State Capitol, which was to be Governor Huey P. Long's great personal monument. This very significant building was on the drawing boards at the time I was in the architects' offices. My task was to trace the details of the toilet stalls.

Periodically Governor Long would visit the office and tour the drafting room, encouraging everyone to complete the plans for the Capitol as soon as possible. On two occasions as he patrolled the rows of drafting tables, he stopped by to acknowledge my existence, and since I was by far the youngest person in the drafting room, he spent a few moments to encourage me and tell me how important it was to him that my drawings be as accurate as possible. He was a very flamboyant and charismatic person, known as The Kingfish, and I remember with fondness these two encounters with Gover-nor—and later, Senator—Huey P. Long, when he took time to visit with me at my drawing board.

I entered Tulane University at the age of seventeen and enrolled in the School of Architecture. At that time the architectural school was a part of the engineering college, and we were required to take a number of engineering courses. For me it was a wonderful revelation to learn how one calculated structures and how buildings were designed. We were also required to take a foreign language, and all of the architects were expected to study French, a holdover from the old tradition that all great architecture originated from the Beaux Art tradition in Paris.

With the exception of one professor, Marion Ross, my experience in the Tulane School of Architecture was not terribly inspiring, the fault basically being my lack of background in the arts. Also, the school curriculum was still very much in the Beaux Art tradition. We had life class, history of art, history of architecture, and structures and design critiques, but no strong design direction or guidance that might have given us the inspiration so important to an architect. But I was fortunate enough to be exposed to some of the greatest architects of our time at Harvard after my stint in the navy.

While I was at Tulane, we were required to measure a historic structure of our choosing, and most of the students selected a building from the many historic sites in the French Quarter. In order to determine what building I would use for

Left: *Clockwise from top left:* Davis, Walter Shepard, John Ladine, Paul Charbonnet, and Walter Binnings, Tulane Architectural School class, mid-1940s.

Below: Mary Henriette Wineman, Davis's wife.

my measure drawing, I methodically walked the French Quarter, passing many Creole cottages with full-length French shuttered windows, some of which were houses of prostitution where the young ladies of pleasure talked to prospective clients through the shutters. A feature of some of these French Quarter cottages was a front stoop where one would find mounds of powdered red brick dust and white substances drawn in patterns. These were voodoo symbols, and I knew that they were important to the occupants, although I did not learn until later that they were related to sexual potency and pornographic enticements. The red brick dust was also believed to protect the owner's home. The symbols did not entice me either to select a building from the French Quarter or to enter the shuttered portals of these houses of pleasure. This was the first time the practice of voodoo came to my attention. It did not occur to me then that it would come to be significant in adventures I would have throughout my life.

For my thesis I actually selected a small chapel in the St. Roch Cemetery, which was built by a priest who had vowed that if his parish were saved from a yellow fever epidemic, he would in appreciation construct a chapel. It was a very unusual stucco-over-brick building with powerful buttresses, a very honest expression of structure. As I discovered through additional research, it was strongly Germanic in inspiration and origin in the tradition of St. Patrick's, a much larger church using similar powerful geometric forms and one of the most imposing edifices in the Central Business District of the city. I admired these two churches very much and truly related to this style. It was somewhat remarkable and prophetic that I would select this small chapel, a structure which was a predecessor in the spirit of Bauhaus architecture, an expression of pure design forms, since later I would be exposed to the strong influence of Walter Gropius, an advocate of the same design philosophy of honesty and purity of form and expression. The St. Roch Chapel is still one of my favorite historic buildings in the city of New Orleans.

While at Tulane, during the summer months I worked as an apprentice architect in a number of local firms, one of which specialized in churches. I was able to actually create the preliminary designs for a number of church edifices. This gave me at a very early age an opportunity to design real buildings in a firm that was quite capable but not terribly creative. At the end of four years at Tulane, I received a Bachelor of Science degree in architecture, and at the end of the fifth year, I was awarded a Bachelor of Architecture degree.

While at Tulane I met a student at Newcomb College, the women's college affiliated with Tulane. Mary Henriette Wineman was originally from Detroit and had come to Newcomb in order to have "a Southern experience." This experience was destined to continue the rest of her life—after her third year of college we were married in her parent's home in Detroit on August 30, 1942. I had completed my fifth year at Tulane; she would receive her B.A. degree during the first year of our marriage while I was still working as an apprentice in a local architectural firm.

At this point, I felt it necessary to obtain more meaningful practical experience. I graduated just after the Pearl Harbor fiasco. World War II was now a reality, and I went to work in Detroit for one of the world's largest architectural firms, Albert Kahn, Inc., which at that time was designing war plants and factories. I was assigned to the structural engineering department and worked under some of the most prestigious structural engineers in the world, many of whom were refugees from Europe, most from Germany. The formulas we used for our structural designs were extracted from textbooks that these very talented engineers had authored before coming to the United States. The opportunity to actually understand structure under such tutelage was a very important part of my education.

All efforts were accelerated for the war. Albert Kahn's office had designed massive wooden structures (since steel was a precious strategic material) to house the construction of flying boats to be used by the navy. My office sent me back to New Orleans to Delta Shipbuilding Company located on Lake Pontchartrain. I was responsible for inspection of the structural members and how they were to be fitted together with bolts and tension rings—all newly created systems which were imaginative solutions to meet the demands of building long-span structures in wood. Being on a construction job was exceedingly gratifying to me. In addition to inspecting the massive wooden trusses, my assignment also required that I set up a transit, an instrument used to determine piling locations for the foundations of the buildings. The setting of the piling locations was very tedious work, made worse by the summer heat radiating from the creosote pilings, burning our skins severely. This, however, was not important—we were sharing in the war effort. Many of the young men my age were being drafted, but as long as I was involved in defense work, I was exempt. During those days I rode to work in a Model A Ford convertible with a rumble seat. It had the simplest, most efficient engine imaginable. There was nothing about that motor which could not be repaired with a screwdriver, a hairpin, and a stick of chewing gum. These were indeed pleasant days for me; however, the military beckoned all young men, and this was the case with me. There was always the constant urge to become more involved in the Great Adventure which was unfolding overseas.

On a number of occasions on the construction job I expressed my desire to get into the war, and one day one of the workers, an elderly Negro laborer who was setting the piling under my direction, informed me if I did go into the service that he would like to do something for me. I told him that I intended to enlist in the Navy, and he said, "Well, tomorrow I will have a gift for you." The next day he returned with a small red oilcloth packet about the size of a large postage stamp, which had been handstitched. To my surprise I discovered he was deeply involved in voodoo.

"Take this with you when you go into the Navy," he instructed. "It will protect you. Don't open it but carry it with you at all times. When you put it in your pocket, if you feel it moving around, don't worry. This will be the charm working." I thanked him for his gift and took the mojo with me into the armed forces.

World War II

There were a number of reasons I chose to serve my country in the navy. I had always been interested in sailboats and sailing. Since my high school days, I had always owned a sailboat of one sort or another. Smaller ones would grow into larger ones, and then later on in life, back to smaller ones—but I had always enjoyed the water, which I believe is reflected in many of my designs. The challenge of the sea seems to be in my blood. As it turned out, my experiences in the navy itself were to be funneled in different directions.

I enlisted and received a commission as an ensign in the United States Naval Reserve and was sent to Dartmouth College for my indoctrination. This was in February, in the middle of one of the coldest winters in recorded history, and for a southern boy who had never seen snow, the experience was exhilarating. One night, acting as the duty officer, I was required to record the temperatures outside and inside the barracks. I entered into the log "48 degrees below zero—exterior" at two o'clock in the morning. But for some reason, I cannot explain it, the southern boys survived this experience in the cold New England winter better than our northern classmates.

For the second time I had attempted to leave Louisiana only to have Fate, this time in the form of the United States Navy, send me back. From Dartmouth I was ordered to return to the Eighth Naval District to learn about camouflage of naval shore installations. I therefore found myself having my anticipated Great Adventure while living in my own home in New Orleans.

We were directed to make elaborate plans for camouflaging naval stations along the coast of the Gulf of Mexico, since there was a considerable amount of submarine activity there. But these were exercises in futility, for none of them were ever realized. After three months at home, I received orders to report to the Bureau of Ships in Washington, D.C., where I was assigned to the Department of Ship Camouflage.

This was indeed fascinating and rewarding work, since we were actually creating designs for the ships of the fleet. With my architectural background, I was able to readily take hold. I learned a great deal about the importance of distorting forms, shade, and shadows, and about the use of color, which later served me in good stead in the practice of architecture. We were working under the guidance of Commander Charles Bittinger, who was involved in ship camouflage during World War I. He had assembled a staff of artists, architects, and engineers, some of whom he had worked with two decades earlier. He was a delightful gentleman in his mid-sixties, who constantly had a long cigar projecting from the very center of his mouth as he shuffled from desk to desk critiquing our designs. We were each assigned specific classes of ships—battleships, aircraft carriers, destroyers, cruisers, tankers, cargo ships, or PT boats, each of which required a different approach to deceiving the enemy. These designs being basic concepts carried over from World War I, many of our theories lost their significance once the Japanese and Germans developed effective radar, but in spite of those limitations, because of the effectiveness of our camouflage designs we were definitely able to achieve our ultimate goal—to limit the casualties through visual deception.

In the beginning I was assigned only auxiliary ships—tankers, troop carriers, and supply ships—but as I became more adept in understanding the system, I was assigned destroyers, cruisers, and finally aircraft carriers and battleships. I was assigned the battleship U.S.S. *Missouri*. I developed a very effective ship camouflage design for painting these massive forms and was sent down to the Brooklyn Navy Yard to assist with the actual painting of the ship. I had no idea what a

Davis in naval uniform and battle fatigues.

monstrous mass the New Jersey Class battleships were until I saw this tremendous hull in dry dock. Using a long stick with chalk on the end, I drew the patterns on the actual hull in accordance with the design I had developed in the studio in Washington. The workmen were somewhat skeptical in the beginning, but they finally took up the challenge of staying within the lines drawn on the hull. Some years later I discovered that the Turkish government issued a postage stamp of the U.S.S. *Missouri* with my camouflage design very much in evidence on the hull of the ship. This stamp is among my prize possessions of World War II. It was on board the "Mighty Mo" that the Japanese surrendered to the U.S. in 1945.

I must admit I was very happy working in Washington at the Bureau of Ships' Camouflage Department and would have stayed there indefinitely; however, the navy sent out an ALLNAV advising the commanders of all departments that officers under the age of twenty-five should be assigned to sea duty or forward-area responsibilities. Commander Bittinger, charged with the task of camouflaging the entire fleet, made a concerted effort to keep me in Washington, as he had only a limited number of people capable of creating these unique designs. Losing a single officer was devastating from his point of view, and he went all the way up the line to the Director of the Bureau of Ships and Director of Na-

Turkish postage stamp of the U.S.S. *Missouri* (the "Mighty Mo") with camouflage design by Davis.

val Personnel. This effort was to no avail, however, and my tour of duty in Washington was cut short. Although I enjoyed my stay in Washington, I was only twenty-two years old and the experience of going to the war zone in the Pacific, viewing the massive assembly of ships in Task Forces, and being a part of the Pacific strikes was worth being exposed to all of the dangers and inconveniences of life at sea. My voodoo charm carried me, thank goodness, through some rather difficult situations, and fate played a part in protecting me through an experience that only those who were there can understand. The grand scale of the United States naval war effort in the Pacific theatre was beyond the comprehension of anyone.

Through the years I have had a number of opportunities to be in close contact with presidents of the United States. In July 1944, I was at Pearl Harbor when President Franklin D. Roosevelt and General Douglas MacArthur met to discuss strategies for the conquering of the main islands of Japan. I happened to be at the site of this crucial meeting when General MacArthur convinced the president to return to the Philippines in order that he might fulfill his prophecy of "I will return."

When I returned to San Francisco, I received an honorable discharge. I must admit this did not cause me any discomfort since I never could adjust to the ways of the military and strongly resented the thought that someone sitting in the Bureau of Personnel in Washington, D.C., was directing my life from his desk. I had never been able to consider myself a naval officer, but rather a civilian in a navy uniform performing duties and receiving orders that seemed totally unrelated to anything that was reasonable or rational.

Some years after the war, when the material related to ship camouflage was declassified, I went to Washington and ferreted out from the files some of the drawings of designs which I had created during my stay at the Bureau of Ships in Washington in 1943. I reproduced them on ship models and prepared a series of lectures explaining the design philosophy of the camouflage of World War II and how it grew out of design concepts developed in World War I.

Harvard

Once again I was thrust into decisions concerning my future in the world of architecture. I had several choices—among them returning to Detroit or New Orleans—but I realized I was not properly prepared to produce the quality of architecture which I felt I was destined to create. I was convinced that I needed additional direction, guidance, and inspiration. These were unusual times—it was the end of the war, and most returning young men were expecting to go back to college under the GI Bill, which was of great assistance in covering tuition and other expenses. I had discovered that Harvard University had enticed Walter Gropius, one of the great architects of our time and founder of the Bauhaus movement, to become chairman of the Graduate School of Design. This was exactly the opportunity for which I had been hoping, but getting into the school was a challenge. There were literally hundreds of applications for admission to the master's course, and Dr. Gropius had determined that he would accept only twelve students for his studio. I returned to New Orleans and applied for the 1945 fall semester. In the meantime I obtained a job as designer in one of the local architectural firms and was given a free hand to develop schematics for their buildings. As luck would have it, I was accepted to the Walter Gropius master's course at Harvard and immediately left New Orleans for Cambridge, Massachusetts.

This experience opened a whole new world for me. During this time at Harvard some of the leading architects of the world were in residence under Dean Hudnutt, but the real inspiration for me was Walter Gropius. Dr. Gropius's assistants were handpicked and were to become some of the most prestigious architects in this country. I worked with and was critiqued by Hugh Stubbins, who later became my client on a very important medical teaching center in Berlin. Another assistant, Chip Harkness, was to be one of the founders of Architects Collaborative, the firm in which Walter Gropius became an active member. The city planning consultant was Walter Wagner; also there was the renowned architect Marcel Breuer. We were permitted to register for specific courses at M.I.T. There Catherine Bauer was developing new techniques for mass housing, and her husband, the famous architect and leader of the Modern Architecture movement, Pietro Belluschi, was the dean. (He later collaborated with Dr. Gropius on the Pan Am Building in New York City.) The faculty Dr. Gropius had gathered around him attracted some of the most talented students from around the world. Of the twelve students in the master's course, six were American and six were from abroad, and I learned a great deal not only from the professors, but also from my fellow students. One of my classmates, I. M. Pei, an undergraduate from M.I.T., eventually became one of the most nationally acclaimed architects of the second half of the twentieth century. His thesis design was a small museum to be built in China—a series of inner courts and gardens with the exhibition space beautifully articulated in a very simple rectangular structure.

These were exciting, invigorating times for me. I felt I was beginning to truly understand architectural design. Walter Gropius emphasized discipline and functionality most vehemently in his critiques of our work. Everything that we did needed to be justified; Gropius left very little room for whimsy or capriciousness. One of our projects was a small library. I decided on a circular structure and attempted to force the functional elements of the building into this shape. As Gropius began his critique of my sketches, his first question was "Why did you decide on a round building?" I replied that I thought I would enjoy the architectural exercise of trying to design a building with this kind of geometric form.

"That is not a good enough reason," Gropius said. "If you want to do a round building, you have to have a need for a round building—not just because you felt that it would be a pleasant experience."

There was always this question of The Reason Why with Dr. Gropius, and I have used it in good stead throughout my entire career, when I would go on to design homes for a diverse group of inhabitants from wealthy socialites to prison inmates. The analytical process justifying my designs has been the yardstick by which I evaluate the quality of our buildings. Many years later I acquired my most unusual and unexpected client, a giraffe at the Audubon Zoo (see page 67). Dr. Gropius would be proud that I finally had a reason to create my round building.

With my background which now included a master's degree from Harvard studying under Walter Gropius, I could pick and choose where I might apply for work. I felt I needed additional experience with prestigious and creative firms. At that time Eero Saarinen in Bloomfield Hills, Michigan, was designing some very exciting buildings. He was one of our most talented architects, following his father Eliel, who was a great influence in the previous generation and who had designed the Cranbrook Institute outside of Detroit where my wife had

Architect Walter Gropius, founder of the Bauhaus School, photographed by Arthur Davis at the time of Gropius's visit to the Davis home on Bamboo Road when Gropius was awarded a Gold Medal by the AIA in New Orleans.

The Beginnings of Curtis & Davis: Residences

About nine months after arriving in Saarinen's office I received a letter out of the blue from Nathaniel "Buster" Curtis, Jr., asking whether I would like to return to New Orleans to form a partnership and open an office there for the practice of architecture. I knew Curtis, but not very well, since he was two classes ahead of me when we were both in the School of Architecture at Tulane. His father, Nathaniel Curtis, Sr., who taught us both, was a very distinguished architect and had a fine reputation as a teacher, designer, and author. He wrote books on the theory of architecture and was very interested in the development of southern architectural traditions.

Buster felt our talents and philosophies were interrelated and thought we could work well together. It was a bit of a gamble to leave Michigan for sleepy New Orleans, but in 1947 that is just what I did.

My partner for the next thirty years was one of the most distinguished, kind, gentle, talented people that I have ever known. He had a wonderful disposition; during the entire length of our partnership we never had any disagreements on design or the operation of our office which could not be resolved expeditiously and with a minimum of friction. One of the reasons we got along so well was that he had a very placid disposition, whereas I was a more volatile, outgoing, even cantankerous person. I have only fond memories of our architectural life together. He was one of the best architectural delineators that I have ever known and could draw beautifully; in fact, he spent a great deal of time doing watercolor drawings of historic buildings, especially Creole cottages and other domestic structures.

Our timing was ideal: After the war, there was a great deal of pent-up demand for buildings in New Orleans, because

attended Kingswood High School. Of special interest was his use of brick and glass as texture, as well as his sense of space—relating landscaping and sculpture to the buildings in a classical way. The school was not only beautiful, but also inspirational for the students who were privileged to learn in such an environment. I decided that if he would accept me, I should go to work in the office of Eero Saarinen. I applied directly after graduation from Harvard and to my surprise and delight, Mr. Saarinen hired me. During this period the Saarinen office was developing a master plan for a research park for General Motors—buildings with beautiful restraint, simple rectilinear forms designed for industrial research but employing glazed brick in a masterful way, juxtapositioned with glass. Those days were quite inspiring for an apprentice, and I was very happy working in Mr. Saarinen's studio.

during the war years there had been little private or municipal construction.

We determined the name of the firm—whether it would be "Curtis & Davis" or "Davis & Curtis"—by the flip of a coin. Nathaniel Curtis won the toss. This worked very well because it was alphabetically correct, and we became known as "C&D." We had a very small office on Perdido Street and only two employees, one of which was my pregnant wife acting as receptionist, bookkeeper, and stenographer. Although the name of the partnership was determined to be "Curtis & Davis, Architects," we later added "and Engineers." Later still, "Engineers" was dropped and we became "Curtis & Davis Architects and Planners."

Curtis and I agreed that we should commit our practice to the design of contemporary buildings and not archeological, traditional, or pseudo-traditional architecture. I was fresh out of Harvard and my immersion in the Bauhaus/Gropius philosophy made me determined to create structures that spoke of my era, not bygone times. Curtis shared this vision. But we were unique. Most of the architects in the South were doing traditional architecture at that time, and in New Orleans, there really were no modern buildings, not in the true sense. Even a flat-roofed house was revolutionary, but we felt the city was ready for modern designs. We would either sink or swim on the premise that we would be known as "modern" architects. We promoted the idea that we were young architects wanting to do contemporary architecture in New Orleans.

We were going in a new direction, and we had to have the kind of clients that would relate to that. During the first year we designed trellises and small shops and even remodeled closets and bathrooms. One of our first designs was a garden trellis based on a Piet Mondrian painting, and even that was shocking to some who saw it. We also were experimenting with flat-roofed houses, as well as butterfly roofs and the use of traditional materials in a fresh, contemporary way. Since our designs were somewhat revolutionary for that time, we received a great deal of publicity in the local newspapers and periodicals. Fortunately for everyone concerned, clients did come and our practice expanded rapidly. It was necessary to take on more employees, and my wife was able to retire to have our first son, Arthur Quentin Davis, Jr.

In strange ways Fate continued to control the direction of my life, and one of the most important commissions I was ever to receive was very small—that of a garden and swimming pool for Edgar B. Stern, Jr. He was a dear friend and be-

Facing page: Curtis and Davis with model of Sako Clinic.

Below: Announcement of the opening of Curtis and Davis Architects and Associated Engineers, 1947.

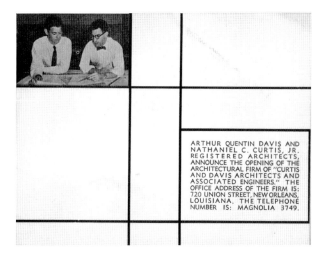

ARTHUR QUENTIN DAVIS AND NATHANIEL C. CURTIS, JR. REGISTERED ARCHITECTS, ANNOUNCE THE OPENING OF THE ARCHITECTURAL FIRM OF "CURTIS AND DAVIS ARCHITECTS AND ASSOCIATED ENGINEERS." THE OFFICE ADDRESS OF THE FIRM IS: 720 UNION STREET, NEW ORLEANS, LOUISIANA. THE TELEPHONE NUMBER IS: MAGNOLIA 3749.

Davis and son Arthur Q. Davis, Jr.

came one of my most cherished and faithful clients. He had recently purchased 6 Garden Lane, a one-story, unassuming house on the edge of the city just inside Orleans Parish but adjoining the exclusive, leafy suburb of Old Metairie. The jewel was the property, not the house. It was approximately two acres, quite deep and heavily wooded with mature trees. Edgar asked me to design a swimming pool to be built in his rear yard which would incorporate the water into the vista from the living and dining rooms. This was a real challenge since the site had specimen cypress and live oaks. My objective was to avoid damaging any of the trees while creating a swimming pool which seemed to belong in this beautiful, semi-tropical setting.

"Do you want a swimming pool, or something really exceptionally interesting?" I asked Edgar.

"It's up to you," he said.

I felt that a geometric pool would not be the proper solution and decided the pool should meander through the trees. Since the shape was sinuous, we used an ordinary garden hose to define the perimeter of the water line. Edgar approved, but suggested that his mother, Edith Stern, who had constructed a magnificent Southern-style mansion at the terminus of his street, should come over to view the concept for the pool before we began construction. Mrs. Stern, Sr., whose parents were the founders of Sears-Roebuck & Co., was a truly gracious lady with strong opinions, and her views were not to be taken lightly. To our great relief she was delighted with the concept of a body of water rambling through the gardens among the trees. But, she wanted to leave her imprint on the design, and she increased the size of each pond by kicking the hose with her foot. This was alright with me— it only improved the shape of the pool.

The pool project turned out to be a much bigger undertaking than either Edgar or I had imagined. When finished, the pool was beautifully lit at night, becoming an abstract water sculpture. During the daytime it reflected the trees and shrubs in a most romantic fashion (see page 68). It was a huge success and on the strength of our efforts, Edgar later suggested that we might be interested in designing the Royal Orleans, a hotel proposed for family-owned property in the heart of the Vieux Carre. This in turn led to many other hotel projects, and those led to still others. I had no idea at the time that this little commission, a swimming pool in a friend's backyard, would be one of the most important things I would ever do to enhance my career. As our practice expanded, we moved our offices to the third floor of 337 Baronne Street.

Eventually we began to get commissions to do houses. Designing houses is usually the stepping stone to larger projects and in some instances the basis for an entire practice. We were young and ambitious and wanted to do more, but were happy to have a house commission from anyone courageous enough to give us the opportunity. In and around the New Orleans area lovely new neighborhoods were being developed in groves of two-hundred-year-old live oaks, dripping in moss and with all of the romance and charm which one associates with southern, genteel living. In one of these subdivisions west of the city, Dr. Morris Shushan wanted to build a home in a grove of oak trees in an area which was relatively inaccessible at that time. After discussions with us, Dr. Shushan and his wife, who was also a doctor, decided they would be most comfortable in a one-story rambling structure with a tremendous overhanging roof with a low pitch and a deep shade protecting the exterior walls from sun, rain, and other elements. The house was designed with this in mind. It was basically a wood structure with brick surfaces adding stability and texture (see page 69). It weathered beautifully through the years, and even to this day it truly belongs in its setting. The second generation of the same family has continued to enjoy and improve upon this very early Curtis & Davis house.

About this time we were awarded the commission to build a house for Walter B. Moses, Jr., on Audubon Boulevard (see page 70). At the front entry to the house we designed a two-story glass window which illuminated the very dramatic floating stairway. In this stairwell, we were able to create a flowing space beginning at the entry vestibule and extending up into the second-story living area. Even though the house was air conditioned, we elected to have quite high ceilings since the air conditioning would not be taxed because of the overhangs and shielding of the large glass areas on the rear. The stairway was dramatic in its simple, pure beauty of form. To add to its drama we convinced Mr. Moses to obtain an original mobile created by Alexander "Sandy" Calder to float in this dramatic space in the stairwell.

At that time it was possible to entice Calder to undertake a simple commission of this sort, especially in New Orleans, as he enjoyed the city's great cuisine. He created not only the mobile in the stairway but also a bronze stabile on the pristine white stucco wall overlooking the swimming pool. These two art objects became the most dominant visual elements in the house and over the years have become almost as valuable as the house itself.

Sandy Calder came to New Orleans with his wife and teenaged daughter—who was continually in a state of shock over his carefree antics. While he was installing his sculpture, my wife and I spent some delightful days with his family eating and drinking in some of our most renowned restaurants and bistros. He was a tremendous mass of a man, yet at the same time had a pixie-like quality, and it was a real joy to share his wit and joie de vivre. Upon leaving New Orleans, Calder presented my wife and me with a small abstract painting which he produced while dining at our home.

A few other houses we designed were original and creative enough to stimulate considerable discussion in the community and had an impact on our reputation. One residence was to be located on the fringe of the Garden District, one of the oldest and most prestigious areas in the center of the city. Originally developed by white northern affluent families coming to New Orleans, the Garden District was located in the American section, in contrast to the Vieux Carre, which was settled by the French and Spanish. For many years these ethnic groups mingled for the purpose of conducting business and commerce, but seldom socially.

In the Garden District, on a corner site with two tremen-

Curtis and Davis, 1950, reviewing a model for the Immaculate Conception School in Marrero, Louisiana.

dous 150-year-old oak trees, Julian Steinberg and his wife Ina wished to build a family residence. Apparently he had spent a great deal of time in Florida and was very much enamored with the white-roofed pink cottages in the Palm Beach area. He advised us that he would like to build a Florida-type cottage with a white roof. After considerable soul searching and many hours of discussion, we were able to convince him that we should build a house which belonged in New Orleans and not in Palm Beach. He finally acquiesced and permitted us to design one of New Orleans's most unusual and exciting residences, contemporary but still retaining influences of Louisiana traditional architecture (see page 71).

We designed many other residences from 1950 to 1960, and most of them were recognized and received awards from the American Institute of Architects.

Like the Steinberg residence, the home we designed for Mr. and Mrs. William Christovich had a high roof with change in volumes by means of raising and lowering the floor slabs. The house was located on a site overlooking Lake Pontchartrain, but was set behind a high levee protecting the residence from the floods and hurricanes that periodically descend upon this part of the country. In order to see the lake it was necessary to develop a high element with a view over the levee above the main house. We designed a sculptural attic, a free-flowing form encased in fiberglass, projecting out of the main roof structure, permitting the master study, an extension of the living room below, a view of the lake above the levee. The remainder of the rooms opened into a central

patio with a glass-enclosed link connecting the two wings of the house—the front block with the entry vestibule, living room, dining room, and kitchen connected by a floating, elevated bridge to the bedroom block containing the master bedroom and three children's rooms. Here again, we attempted to relate to the interior patios of the old French Quarter houses and, in this case, created an inner garden with a strong Japanese influence, lushly landscaped with a flowing stream, a delightful aspect viewed from both the living room and dining rooms as well as the master bedroom. This house influenced the design of a later residence which I designed for myself.

Public Housing and Schools

By the early 1950s the New Orleans Public Housing Authority had built a number of public housing projects, all based upon the philosophy that the occupants should live in two- and three-story walk-up cottages. Curtis & Davis was selected to design a housing project on a site near the center of the city, adjacent to the central railroad terminal. The site was a relatively narrow, linear property with requirements for a very high density per acre.

To accommodate the number of families to be housed on the site, we believed that the cottage-courtyard plan would be inefficient and eliminate almost any possibility for open playground areas. We therefore attempted to approach the design with the concept that the larger two- and three-bedroom units for families would open directly out onto play areas and open gardens. To meet the densities expected, we would accommodate the elderly and the young occupants without families in a high-rise apartment building, similar to the kind of public housing that was prevalent in densely populated areas in many of the northern cities, especially in and around New York City. Stacking these units would open the site and create the kind of recreation-oriented open plan sorely needed in the very congested area of the city.

This was a rather revolutionary approach, since the Housing Authority of New Orleans had never built any high-rise housing units in the past and was more or less dedicated to the cottage-cluster plan. Officials were concerned as to whether such a "radical" approach should be attempted in the first new public housing project to be built in over twenty years. The Housing Authority requested an opinion from the local chapter of the American Institute of Architects, and a committee was appointed to evaluate our plans. Since the members of the review committee were architects with previous experience in designing earlier public housing developments, they were dedicated to the cottage low-rise approach. They strongly condemned our design and recommended that we should not be permitted to develop a high-rise scheme in New Orleans, arguing that the people who would occupy it were not capable of living in a building with elevators, the layout would stimulate crime, and it would create unnecessary trauma for people who had never lived in anything but two- and three-story buildings. We disagreed and presented livable and quite successful examples of high-rise public housing in many cities throughout the nation. Ultimately irrefutable statistics and our logical analysis of the high-rise/low-rise scheme were so convincing that we carried the day. For a considerable number of years after this confrontation with the local chapter, our firm—and I personally, who took this very much to heart—severed relationships with the chapter. One year later this project received the Honor Award from the American Institute of Architects.

The Housing Authority decided to build our design as a prototype (see page 73). The project still stands as a monument to our tenacity to overcome all objections when we were thoroughly convinced that our design was the proper one. As a result of this stand that we took, low-income families in New Orleans would have an opportunity to live in housing of equal quality to their fellow citizens.

After World War II there was a strong demand for the construction of new school buildings. No school buildings had been constructed for more than five years because of the war, and most of the New Orleans Public Schools were quite old and in deplorable condition. The prewar schools were mostly three-story masses of brick or masonry with stucco. The ground floor in most cases was the "basement," since it was on grade (on ground level) because of soil conditions. It usually included dark and dingy corridors, locker rooms, dining facilities, and meeting areas. A steep monumental stair accessed the second and third levels which typically housed a center hall and four classrooms on each side per level for a total of sixteen classrooms. The stair was wide but very hazardous, and the children were at risk, especially between classes when they would storm up and down these very steep staircases. The exterior fenestration usually consisted of tall double-hung windows—the most desirable thing about the classrooms being that they had very high ceilings, most fourteen to sixteen feet. The students near the windows had satisfactory light on their desks, but because the classrooms were quite deep, those students nearer the corridor were in semi-darkness. The suspended artificial lighting was woefully inadequate.

Since a whole series of schools was to be constructed, we decided to wage a campaign to convince the school board that the new schools should embrace modern concepts of planning including less massive structures, more human scale, relationship between the indoors and outdoors, and acknowledgment of our climatic conditions with appropriate shade, cross ventilation, and open spaces. In one article initiated through an interview with a newspaper reporter, we described the difference between a typical classroom in the "monumental box" and what we envisioned as a low-rise open plan school for the future. We coined a term which became a significant catch phrase for the people who were leaning toward the design of new contemporary school buildings. We pointed out that the children nearest the windows in the existing school structures would have enough light to read and study, but those on the inside of the classroom might very well be handicapped by having insufficient illumination. So we suggested that the article pose the question, "Does your child have a lucky seat?" The "lucky seat" slogan took off and became a rallying cry for a new approach to school architecture in New Orleans.

The president of the school board fortunately was a dynamic, intuitive, creative woman who was sensitive to our point of view. President Jacqueline Leonhard suggested to the board that we be given the opportunity to design the first elementary school as part of the new construction program. The school board was somewhat concerned since we had never completed a school and our reputation was one of not only creative, but also revolutionary approaches. Most of the architecture being built in New Orleans at that time was exceedingly conservative. They agreed to have us design the first elementary school in collaboration with another architectural firm which had a reputation for conservative, sound planning. We readily accepted the suggestion. So, the firm of Douglas Ferret and our own firm collaborated on the first school, which was not very revolutionary (see page 74). It was the first one-story school building built in New Orleans that we know of in this last century. It started the trend toward low, open school planning which had also been developed in Texas by some very creative architects under the direction of Bill Caudil at Caudil, Rowlette, Scott.

Since the school was well received, we were given another school on our own, the Thomy Lafon Elementary School, and this was one of our most exciting and creative designs (see pages 75–76). The site was a long, thin property in the center of a federal public housing project. Our idea was to have an outdoor covered play area, cross ventilation, and all of the classrooms at one level. As the site was being prepared for construction, caskets and tombs were unearthed. The Archbishop had to be summoned to deconsecrate the ground and the burial remains had to be relocated. This school was very well received by the students, faculty, and school board. The American Institute of Architects awarded it the First Honor Award for the Best and Most Creative School in the Country. We considered it a landmark and an important contribution to the design of the contemporary school buildings for the Deep South.

Unfortunately, a later school board added a wing and awnings, completely ruining the original concept.

One of the largest educational institutions designed by our firm was the George Washington Carver Elementary, Junior, and Senior High School (see page 77). The Orleans Parish School Board commissioned us to design a senior high school on a large tract of land of approximately fifty acres. A portion of the site was to be set aside for a junior high which would be designed by another architect, and perhaps later another portion of the site would be spun off for an elementary school. We advised the school board that we did not believe that this was the most practical or expeditious way to use the site. If the junior and senior highs could be combined, they could share kitchen and cafeteria facilities and have one first-class auditorium instead of two smaller, less useful ones. A small auditorium could not provide a stage loft and the backstage area needed for a first-class high school auditorium—one which could also be available to the

Moscow Adventure

After its construction, articles about the Lafon School were published in architectural journals in the United States and abroad, and it was chosen to be part of an exposition held in Moscow in 1959 featuring significant aspects of the American culture. I was asked to assist in planning the exhibition. The United States Trade and Cultural Fair, which covered approximately five acres in Sokolinki Park, was beautifully conceived. There was a geodesic dome, with ramps and platforms floating in the space under the dome. The exhibition featured kiosks of books and popular American magazines describing life in the United States.

The education area featured schools and universities of special significance, the Lafon School was given a very prominent setting. The entrance presented a twelve-foot-long by eight-foot-high billboard depicting a portion of the façade of the two-story classroom wing of our revolutionary elementary school. The photograph was very dramatic, featuring not only the building, but also the children at play in front of the kindergarten ramp and the abstract sculpture with children climbing over the surfaces of the six-foot-high Henry Moore–inspired statue, placed in the center of the children's playground.

community for evening productions. The same would apply to the gymnasiums. We could build a much larger and much more efficient gymnasium if it were to serve the two schools.

We submitted to the school board our proposal for combining the cafeteria, kitchen, auditorium, and gymnasium and proved to them that we could save a few million dollars while at the same time having a much more efficient complex (see page 77). We also proposed a central mechanical system, rather than two separate ones. The school board saw the wisdom of our proposals and agreed to let us design this important campus incorporating the junior and senior highs, and later they decided to go forward with the elementary school.

One difficulty gave us a great deal of discomfort. We were awarded the senior high school after the Douglas Ferret firm—the same firm with whom we collaborated on the first modern school—was awarded the junior high school. Of course, they were upset that this commission had been taken away from them. We asked Mrs. Leonhard to consider using Mr. Ferret's firm for another junior high in another location in order that he would not be penalized for our good fortune. He was awarded another school, and our campus design won an award from the American Institute of Architects as the Best Overall Master Plan for a School Complex for 1957. Although it won a First Design Award for Progressive Architecture Design, the beautiful double arches of the cafeteria and the auditorium for the junior and senior high have now been closed by chainlink fences and barbed wire to prevent the students from climbing onto the roof of the building and vandalizing the structure. Unfortunately the play areas have also been fenced off into small parcels, creating an almost prison-like atmosphere.

We were given a commission to design, in the center of Harlem, on 126th Street and Madison Avenue in Manhattan, a junior high school which proved to be a very important symbol and a revolutionary design for the City of New York school system (see page 78). Harlem had experienced tremendous problems with the breakage of glass windows and other vandalism. Our design for Intermediate School 201 certainly solved that problem. We created a windowless school raised on piers off the ground, similar to the Thomy Lafon School. Since it was in the center of a depressed neighborhood, the area beneath was to become the playground for the entire area.

Another somewhat revolutionary feature of the design was placing the cafeteria, the gymnasium, and the arts and crafts facilities underground, further freeing the ground level acreage for outdoor recreation. It was our intention in placing them on a different level that these facilities would be used not only by the school but also by the neighborhood. There were no community centers in this part of Harlem and the use of a cafeteria/auditorium for stage and recreational events would have been a very useful asset to the community. This part of the school was designed with separate access from the street so that after school hours these amenities could remain open without disturbing the security of the school.

Since there were no windows on the exterior walls, vandalism was reduced and the classrooms were able to expand and contract. The walls between the classrooms were non-structural and designed to be readily moved. None of the walls have ever been changed or relocated, and all of the facilities that were designed to be used by the community to the best of my knowledge have never been made available for community use. It is our sincere hope that an enlightened school board and imaginative principal will yet use the facilities of this unique school to their full potential.

In addition to these schools, we were commissioned to design university campuses and college buildings, including the Science Building at Tulane University (see page 79), and the entire master plan for the newly founded University of New Orleans campus, including classroom buildings, the ecumenical center, and the arts, music, and drama building. We also designed an elementary school in Stanford, Connecticut, and a campus plan for all of the buildings at the New York Institute of Technology.

Of Sunscreens and Saigon:
Healthcare Facilities and Federal Buildings

The Sako Clinic, a very small clinic for the practice of pediatric medicine, was significant to our practice because of innovative techniques we developed in its design. It was designed for a doctor with Japanese ancestry. Incorporating the classical architecture of Japan, we designed a very simple, rectilinear building with an oriental courtyard at the entrance. It is in Raceland, Louisiana, near the delta of the Mississippi River. Because the area flooded regularly, we raised the clinic four feet off the ground. It was accessible by two ramps leading up to the garden entrance. Since the vertical pier supporting the building was recessed, the rectangle shape appeared to float above the flat terrain of the Mississippi delta (see page 80).

It was on this project that we made our first attempt to

use the masonry screen element, in this case constructed of terra cotta flue tile. The building was beautiful in its simplicity and was our first use of clay tile. We used the same technique for a small twenty-five-bed hospital built in the town of Tallulah, Louisiana, in Madison Parish and for our own office building on Canal Street (see page 81). We created façades with sun screens of different materials and configurations for the American Embassy in Saigon, the George Washington Carver Junior and Senior High Schools, and the Berlin Medical Center. We also included an elaborate aluminum sun screen for the main branch of the New Orleans Public Library.

A small project can become the impetus for major commissions. Our involvement with healthcare architecture began with the Sako Clinic. It was followed by a series of small Hill-Burton hospitals, twenty-five to fifty beds. At that time the federal government provided incentives to finance these small hospitals throughout the country. We designed a few of these facilities with the intent that they could be effi-

ciently expanded as the demand dictated. The small hospitals we designed in Lutcher, Madison Parish, and St. James Parish were well received and showcased extensively in architectural magazines. We went on to complete such major projects as the Lakewood Hospital in New Orleans; the Edna Pillsbury Clinic; the Towbin Healthcare Center, a veterans hospital in North Little Rock, Arkansas; the Science Center at Tulane University; the Science Center at the Medical Center in Nashville, Tennessee; the United States Naval Hospital at the naval base in Algiers, Louisiana; and research laboratories for the Ochsner Medical Foundation in New Orleans.

Our firm also designed a number of federal projects. The General Services Administration contracted us to design a Department of Defense building on Independence and 10th Street in Washington, D.C., presently known as the James V. Forrestal Building. The Office of Foreign Buildings for the State Department selected us to design the United States Embassy in Saigon prior to the Vietnam War. The National

Institute of Health commissioned us, along with an engineering firm from Omaha, Nebraska, and a minority Washington firm, to design the Ambulatory Care and Research Center at the National Institute of Health in Bethesda, Maryland.

At that time all of the major government buildings on Independence were large masonry blocks in either marble or limestone. We decided that the James V. Forrestal Building would introduce a new vocabulary, one in which the solid mass and ponderous block would be replaced by a linear graceful, rectilinear floating element. All public buildings in Washington, D.C., must be reviewed by the Fine Arts Commission, which was composed of a series of architects, planners, and government officials. Our building, which was somewhat revolutionary for a federal office building, was scrutinized extensively by the Fine Arts Commission. The Department of Defense, frustrated by months of debate, proposals, and counterproposals, pressed for a resolution. Finally we agreed to a fenestration framed in precast concrete elements, but we were still able to greatly increase the glassed areas and to some extent preserve the integrity of our original design concept (see pages 82–83).

Having to defend our design was costly for us, delaying the project almost four months and requiring us to make innumerable additional drawings. As with other projects, we have always defended our designs when we were convinced that what we were proposing was the right solution.

The Towbin Healthcare Center for the Veterans Administration Hospital in North Little Rock was a major commission for our firm and, with the exception of the Berlin Medical Center, the largest medical complex we have designed (see page 84). We were selected along with Nolan Blass Architects, a very distinguished local Arkansas firm. The hospital was made up of eight pavilions built around a central quadrangle, with the administration in a separate pavilion at one end. The program presented to us required that we renovate the pavilions which could be salvaged, and three that were beyond repair should be demolished and replaced by new pavilions. Our budget was approximately $55 million, and we developed a design which could accommodate the program and easily stay within the budget. It was obvious to us, however, that this was not the proper solution. We told the VA that for the same amount of money we could demolish all of the pavilions with the exception of two that could be renovated for Special Care and build a modern hospital on the site. The VA did not want to delay the project, but if at our own risk we wished to prepare an alternate design and cost estimate, they would be willing to entertain our alternate scheme. When we presented our design, we finally were authorized to proceed with our centralized hospital design. Happily it came in within the money—with a few million dollars to spare, and now North Little Rock has a Veterans Administration Hospital with the most advanced planning techniques in a very handsome building.

The National Institute of Health asked us to design an Ambulatory Care and Research addition to an eight-hundred-bed hospital while not disturbing the existing building during the construction. The hospital was built in the thirties and was as efficient as hospitals built at that time could possibly be. We explored seven different solutions to link the hospital to the new research center and, using a design matrix, evaluated the merits and shortcomings of each one by point system. We presented the entire analysis to the director and the medical board, explaining how each of these solutions could function. Through this analytical process we convinced the medical director that the design should be a solid block connecting to the hospital at every level by enclosed bridges. The resulting building not only functions exceedingly well, satisfying difficult program requirements, but also is a de-

lightful building for the staff and outpatients of the Ambulatory Care and Research Center (see pages 85–86).

Another important government commission was the United States Embassy in Saigon, Vietnam, before the outbreak of hostilities in that country. In 1950 I was dispatched to meet with the United States ambassador to Vietnam at that time, Frederick Reinhardt, a distinguished public servant. He had served in Moscow, spoke fluent Russian, and had been sent to Saigon despite the fact that he was one of the most knowledgeable State Department diplomats on the situations in Russia. The entire city of Saigon, on the Saigon River, smelled pungently of fish, day and night. Since fish was a staple of their diet, it was served in numerous ways, all very odorous and in some instances almost revolting.

We stayed at a very old hotel, the Majestic, and the conditions were primitive. The hotel kept lizards on the ceiling in order to collect mosquitoes and other bugs. I had never thought of lizards as a mosquito repellant.

Ambassador Reinhardt and I discovered that our approach to the design of the embassy was compatible, and we spent many pleasant evenings together analyzing what should be built in Vietnam. I had done a considerable amount of research on the history and culture of the country. Most of the existing buildings showed influences from either France, China, Cambodia, or India, but I found nothing of significance that we could use as an inspirational for the design of the embassy.

Since the embassy was to be a seven-story structure and in a tropical climate, we decided to use a sun screen to protect the exterior walls from direct sun and torrential rains. In this instance, it would also add security as a formidable barrier against intrusion. This design decision was prophetic. This sun screen would later protect the building during the Viet Cong attacks on the embassy compound.

When we began our planning, the French were evacuating Vietnam shortly after the Dien Bien Phu catastrophe in the spring of 1954, and now it appeared that the United States was about to fall into the same trap. We completed the design drawings, and at the precise moment that hostilities were commencing, we were prepared to begin the construction. We had selected a contractor who, as it turned out, was also forced to evacuate Vietnam, and the completion of the building was actually accomplished by United States Navy Seabee battalions (see page 87). The embassy became very famous when the helicopters landed on the roof for evacuation when Saigon fell on April 30, 1975. Though we did not foresee these circumstances, the structure was designed to accommodate such peak loads. Photographs of this historic event graphically depict our building standing strong against enemy intrusions (see page 88). When the North Vietnamese took over Saigon, the building was demolished.

Sinners and Saints

After meeting Huey Long as a teenager, the next governor with whom I had direct personal contact was Robert F. Kennon (term 1952–1956), who desired to build a model state penitentiary, "second to none in the country," at Angola. He was a very religious man, and as a prelude to most of our conferences, he would begin with a short prayer that our efforts would be fruitful and in accordance with God's wishes. This was impressive for me, since I have never had such an experience in dealing with a politician before. Governor Kennon gave us his full support and encouragement and advised us that at no time would he tolerate kickbacks of any sort. He wanted our design to be the best possible with the funds available.

The Louisiana State Penitentiary at Angola at that time had a horrible reputation as being one of the most brutal, cruel, and poorly equipped facilities in the United States. The inmates were constantly at odds with the custodial staff, the food was atrocious, and the accommodations were below acceptable standards. To visually express their protests against the living conditions, the inmates were cutting their tendons and disfiguring themselves in other ways to gain the attention of the public and the administration in Baton Rouge. *Life* magazine had devoted almost an entire issue to the horrendous conditions at Angola. The governor had resolved that Louisiana must build a modern facility to replace this terrible complex, which was referred to by *Life* as "the hellhole of the nation, only to be surpassed by Devil's Island and the chain gangs of Georgia."

Governor Kennon asked us to determine what was necessary to build one of the finest prisons in the country. The director of the Federal Bureau of Prisons, James V. Bennett, a remarkable man and first-class administrator, was the person with whom we began our research. His theories of incarceration, education, and rehabilitation would be the cornerstone of the design philosophy for our modern correctional institution. We spent many hours in Washington with Mr. Bennett and visited federal institutions that he felt would give us the background we should have. He directed us to some of the best and some of the worst institutions in the federal system as well as some state institutions. The most significant contribution Mr. Bennett made, however, was to suggest that we employ the services of Reed Cozard, one of his top administrators, who agreed to come to Louisiana and work with us during planning, construction, and setting up of the operation of the "New Angola."

While we were planning the new institution, the state correctional administration also developed a new statewide system for classifying inmates for maximum-, medium-, and minimum-security housing. Once we understood how a humane correctional institution should be built, we developed a design that was so simple, straightforward, and honest in concept that it almost designed itself (see pages 89–92).

Mr. Bennett and Mr. Cozard were as interested in attempts to rehabilitate the inmates as they were in securing the institution from escape attempts. We created an industrial compound where inmates were permitted to work in factories built at the site. State automobile license plates were manufactured at Angola, and much of the furniture for state institutions was designed and built there. There were fabrication plants for other state facilities and electrical and mechanical workshops where inmates were able to learn a trade. The new facility also had classrooms where inmates, many of whom were illiterate, had an opportunity to learn to read and write. An institutional newspaper became quite famous since some of the inmates were exceedingly talented writers, and the editor was an ex-newspaperman who produced editorials of the highest quality.

For the dormitory units, the floor slab and the roof—

which had both been poured on the ground—were hydrauli-cally jacked into place (see plage 24a). The roof was welded onto the column at an elevation of twelve feet and the floor slab jacked to a three-foot level, which became the estab-lished height for all of the walkways, thus protecting both the dormitory units and the connecting walkways from the tor-rential rains, flooding, and unstable ground conditions which are prevalent throughout this area. With the two slabs in place, the plumbing, the nonstructural concrete block walls, and the exterior fenestration were installed. The dormitory designs for minimum and medium security were so simple and so straightforward that we recommended that the in-mates themselves complete their own housing units, provid-ing an opportunity for them to learn a trade. Since there were large numbers of housing clusters, the institution agreed to experiment with assigning half of the housing units to the in-mates who would be furnished with all of the necessary ma-terials and instructional help, while the other half would be built by contractors. As it turned out, this concept was highly successful, and in many instances, the inmates were able to install the interior partitions and enclose the buildings 10 to 15 percent faster than the general contractors. This became a source of great pride to them. The entire institution was completed on schedule and under budget. Mr. Cozard spent the next two years working with the administrative staff to insure that the facility was used in the way that it had been conceived on the drawing board.

The main prison complex was completed in 1955 and re-ceived a great deal of praise from members of the prison in-dustry, especially Mr. Bennett, director of the Federal Bureau of Prisons. The architectural design was reported extensively in American architectural publications and in 1956 received a First Honor Award from the American Institute of Architects. The publicity brought us quite a few additional opportuni-ties to design correctional institutions around this country, and we even consulted the British government on prisons proposed in the British Isles. After the experience of Angola, I discovered that I was not personally interested in pursuing correctional work. Most of the other prisons which our firm designed were planned by Curtis or other architects in our office, and although from time to time I critiqued the design concepts, I did not have the in-depth involvement that I had with Angola. Curtis & Davis ultimately designed thirty-eight correctional institutions, among them the award-winning Washington Correction Center in Washington, D.C., the Nas-sau County Jail, and the Illinois State Penitentiary.

In a radical turnaround, some of our most satisfying com-missions were our church designs, all of which have been Catholic. This is somewhat difficult to explain since neither Curtis nor I are Catholics. Our first church design was in the small New Orleans suburb of Marrero on the West Bank of the Mississippi River. The Immaculate Conception parish was not the most affluent, and the seating capacity of the church was only three hundred people. The final design was quite beautiful in its utter simplicity and honest expression of the use of exposed natural materials (see pages 94–95).

In Lake Charles we were given the opportunity to design a church on a lovely site heavily wooded with second-gener-ation pine trees, tall, linear, and graceful. We decided that the church should nestle into its surroundings but at the same time be strong enough to make a strong spiritual statement. The pastor of Our Lady Queen of Heaven Church was very adventurous and was receptive to a dramatic, perhaps even theatrical, environment in which he could literally create images for his practitioners by means of projections from a concealed clear story. The church was a one-story structure, enclosed completely by a twelve-foot-high white brick wall (see page 97).

Davis with daughter Pam and son Quint.

We had originally designed the seating with a central aisle and a conventional nave similar to the one that we had employed at the Marrero church. But the pastor of Our Lady Queen of Heaven wanted to change the relationship between the congregation and the altar. He wished to bring the people in closer and create more of an amphitheater configuration for the seating. In order to accomplish this, we designed the seating area as more of a square than an elongated rectangle (see page 96), with the altar projecting out into the seating area. The church was devoid of any ornament other than the exposed natural surfaces. But with a clear story over the altar and a solid panel above the altar under the clear story, the pastor was able to achieve one of his objectives—to project images over the altar before, during, and after the mass, adding more drama and creating a sensation of spiritual well being. We expanded on this concept of seating "in the round" in the design of our next, largest, and most impressive Catholic church, St. Frances Cabrini in New Orleans (see pages 98–101).

Home Life

As the firm achieved greater success, I designed homes for my own family, all of which received awards from the American Institute of Architects. Each time we built a house, we had another child. My wife Mary and I had two boys and a girl. I began designing the second home as we worked at Angola and used the lift-slab construction there as well.

My oldest son, Arthur Q. "Quint" Davis, Jr., has become quite a famous producer of jazz festivals. In New Orleans he created the New Orleans Jazz and Heritage Festival, or Jazz Fest, which is the largest festival of its kind in the world. He has also produced festivals in other cities throughout the United States and Europe. My daughter Pam is happily married, a real joy, and a delightful human being. James, our third child and second son was in the contracting business, married to Jill, a charming young lady, and produced three children: Elizabeth, Matthew, and Christopher—our only grandchildren. The great tragedy of our lives was that James through a freak accident was killed as he was attempting to prune a large oak tree in his garden adjacent to his home. This house was also designed by me and his widow, who is

James and Jill, June 1979.

now remarried to Michael Botnick. He is a fine man and we are happy to have him as part of our family.

In the early fifties, I acquired a site near Lake Pontchartrain in a subdivision known as Lake Vista, which was laid out as a series of cul-de-sacs. I selected a double lot opening onto a green belt that penetrated the entire subdivision. The green belt was oriented to the south, giving the house an ideal exposure with quite a large expanse of open green fields. My design successfully integrated the gardens and interior spaces (see pages 102–3). I sold the home to a local pediatrician, who has maintained the house very well.

Our second home, on Bamboo Road, was presented with a First Honor Award from AIA for residential design (see pages 104–7). When my mentor Walter Gropius attended the national conference of the American Institute of Architects in New Orleans to receive the Gold Medal, he visited our home for dinner. He commented on the fact that this residence was expressive of the disciplines which he hoped he had instilled in us. He especially appreciated the textures and colors, and the warmth created through the use of traditional materials. Those kind words from Dr. Gropius meant more to me than any honor awards I have received.

By coincidence I found out I had inherited a Bourbon Street house at the same time that I received a handsome cash offer for my Bamboo Road home, which was by then too large for our family. Two of my three children were grown. We seemed destined to move to Bourbon Street.

I've owned several homes and loved each one, but there is something special about the house at 1440 Bourbon Street (see page 108). The house had been most recently owned by

Louis Clapp, the same gentleman who assisted us in the development of the floor plan and detailing for the Moses residence on Audubon Boulevard. He lived on Bourbon Street with his wife until she passed. He continued to live there alone until he bequeathed the home to me some years later. We had become close friends and he had no relatives in the area.

Built between 1790 and 1810 by the carpenter Jean-Louis Dolliole, a "free man of color," the Bourbon Street cottage was one of the oldest and best preserved still in existence in the Vieux Carre. It survived the many fires, floods, and hurricanes that have swept through New Orleans in the last two hundred years. During the thirties, the building was part of the historic renovations initiated by the Works Progress Administration to provide employment for architects. In 1934 the cottage was meticulously measured by Sam Wilson, a local architect.

When the house passed into my hands, it needed extensive remodeling, but it was very important that it was restored properly. Sam Wilson's drawings proved invaluable in this regard. The Library of Congress had preserved the plans which were available to us and assisted us with our renovations. The original house was a cottage with two large rooms, a porch, and a kitchen; we expanded by adding three bedrooms and a carport. The original exterior of the cottage was yellow cement stucco over wooden posts. The expansion of the house required a different material, but we wanted one that would blend with the original design. Our addition did not in any way conflict with the original materials of the cottage. I had a friend who owned one of the large plantations up the river, San Francisco Plantation. There were a number of slave quarters he intended to demolish at about the time that we were doing the restoration. From one of the buildings, he gave us the original cypress boards, one inch thick by twelve to fifteen inches wide. These timbers were untreated but had a beautiful patina, and they became the exterior surfaces of the addition to the cottage. Although the materials were different, the wood boards blended harmoniously with the original stucco.

The bedroom addition stretched from one side of the original cottage to the back of the deep lot. On the other side of the cottage we added the carport. Out back we built a Japanese stone garden and a swimming pool and preserved much of the exiting foliage, including a seventy-five-year-old willow, several magnolias, and fruit-bearing fig trees. From the backyard the addition looks like two rustic cottages, even though it's really one long addition.

And therein lies its essence: The house is true to itself and to its time. It is highly functional and yet pleasing to the eye. There is something truly magical about it. The cottage was extensively photographed by *Architecture Digest*, and a complete description of the history of the building was included.

Hotels and Playboy Clubs

The small commission at the beginning of my career for a garden and swimming pool for a personal friend led to a dramatic expansion of the practice of Curtis & Davis. Edgar B. Stern, Sr., owned a site in the French Quarter facing St. Louis Street and bounded by Royal and Chartres Streets—a prime French Quarter location. He decided a first-class hotel in the Vieux Carre would be a sensible business venture as well as a contribution to the community. In 1957 Edgar Stern, Sr., and Roger Sonnabend (Chairman of Hotel Corporation of America, now Sonesta International Hotels) issued a joint statement in the New Orleans *States* that they were going to build the hotel. Edgar Stern, Jr., well satisfied with the very unusual development of his swimming pool and its integration with

the lush vegetation of his landscaped garden, recommended that our firm be given this incredible opportunity. I must say that this was very brave of Edgar since not only had we never done a hotel, we had never designed a building of this scope and magnitude. It was destined to cover half an entire city block in the very heart of the oldest section of the city. Edgar, Jr., sold his father and Roger Sonnabend on letting me have this chance to design their hotel, which was also a very brave thing for *them* to do—perhaps even foolhardy.

At the time, the site was a vacant piece of land devoted to parking. The only construction was on the Chartres Street side where there was a series of free-standing, two-story granite arches that were at one time a part of another, very historic hotel erected on this same site in the 1830s. The St. Louis Hotel was the location of a number of historic events related to the development of the city. Before the Civil War, slaves were sold in the rotunda under a great domed roof in the main lobby of the hotel, and during the war, Confederate Congress met there on at least one occasion. The hotel experienced two major fires, the first of which destroyed the entire dome. Subsequently the hotel was rebuilt and a new dome was erected, but this time constructed of terra cotta pots which were linked one to the other—a structurally sound concept and an ingenious way to build a dome which would be completely fireproof. Before the turn of the century the hotel was plagued by still another fire and the entire building was destroyed with the exception of the granite arches at Chartres Street. One of our earliest decisions was to decide how to use these arches in the new hotel, thereby creating a visual link from the old St. Louis Hotel to the new Royal Orleans Hotel (see pages 109–10).

In our plan the lower floor on the main façade facing the street echoed the granite columns of the original St. Louis Hotel but was constructed in masonry covered in plaster. The original granite arches were removed from the site but were properly labeled and numbered so that they could be erected once again after the frame of the hotel had been completed. To this day they stand in the exact location where they were originally built as the exterior corner of the original St. Louis Hotel. We left them in their natural state and they are an integral part of the hotel design facing Chartres Street. This final design was approved by the Vieux Carre Commission.

There was a great deal of public concern as to whether a hotel of any sort, and especially of this size—proposed as 350 rooms—could be a financial success. Lester Kabacoff, an assistant to Mr. Stern, who would become a major New Orleans developer himself, moved the project forward, and through his tenacious efforts, it was completed and proved to be a success. Mr. Stern formed a new corporation, Royal St. Louis, with a number of affluent citizens in the community making up its board of directors and furnishing the necessary equity capital required to finance the hotel.

The hotel needed sufficient off-street parking for hotel guests as well as for guests attending events. The insurance company financing the hotel in concert with Royal St. Louis required a parking structure that would accommodate at least 350 cars. The Vieux Carre Commission demanded that the façade of the parking garage blend into the architecture of the hotel as well as the other buildings on the block. Mr. Stern fortunately also owned the property next door, the original home of WDSU television station and its famous Broulatour Courtyard, so we were not only able to incorporate arches and shuttered fenestration in keeping with the hotel, but also modify the adjoining property to visually harmonize with the proposed garage.

The hotel opened with a gala celebration on October 8, 1960, and within the first year the occupancy was beyond the projections, and the owners wanted to add another fifty rooms. Luckily the roof we designed could carry the load of an additional floor, so we recommended that the six-story, flat-roof structure add a sloping mansard-type roof with separate dormer windows in each room, a feature that was truly in the French Quarter tradition. The rooms were designed with sloping walls and a dormer large enough to actually enter and look down upon the rooftops of the Vieux Carré. This gave the rooms a flavor of a Paris studio. We were granted permission to exceed the height limit of French Quarter buildings because we were building to the height of the original hotel on the site, the historic St. Louis Hotel. The extra floor added in 1963 appears to have always been a part of the original design.

This first hotel commission led to others in the city, including the Royal Sonesta Hotel (see page 111) for the same client and the same operator, and additional hotels in New Orleans for Marriott and Hyatt. The Hyatt Hotel became the focal point for the master plan for an entire square adjacent to the Louisiana Superdome, which our firm later designed.

It is unusual for an architect to design more than one building for a client, but on the strength of the swimming pool for Edgar B. Stern, Jr., we were asked to design our first hotel, the Royal Orleans; the second hotel, the Royal Sonesta; the third hotel, the Stanford Court in San Francisco (see pages 112–13); a condominium village in Park City, Utah; and then a new community in an existing oil field in Huntington Beach, California—all thanks to my friend Edgar. Our first hotel, managed by Hotel Corporation of America under the guidance of Roger Sonnabend, paved the way for a relationship in which the Sonnabend group asked us to design not only the Royal Sonesta in New Orleans, but also hotels in Cambridge, Massachusetts, and Lynn, Massachusetts; renovations to the famous Plaza Hotel in New York; and hotels in Europe—all of this from a swimming pool in a friend's backyard in New Orleans, Louisiana.

We also created designs for hotels that were never built. There were two overseas designs, one in Taipei for a general who was the son of Chiang Kai-shek. He along with Robert Anderson, former secretary of the treasury, had obtained a site in downtown Taipei. We designed a truly exciting hotel on a very difficult lot, but for political and other reasons beyond our control, the hotel was never constructed. The same thing happened in Cairo when we developed designs for a Ramada Hotel facing the Nile on the west bank (see page 114).

In the sixties and seventies Playboy mania was in full swing. The magazine was exceedingly popular and on the strength of that popularity Hugh Hefner decided to create a three-dimensional *Playboy* magazine in the form of quasi-private clubs with a theme similar to that of the magazine. Playboy Clubs became as popular as the magazine itself. Private investors would fund the clubs—which Hefner's organization would operate—and share the profits, except for the original Playboy Club in Chicago. Several big cities were designated as potentially sound locations; many places were staked out but not all were actually chosen. New Orleans was among those original ones because of the image of a freer society here and a site in the French Quarter was available. The Playboy organization selected a local manager, Peter Moss, who was an assistant manager at the Roosevelt Hotel, the largest hotel in the city at that time. He was the nephew of Seymour Weiss, who owned the hotel, and had excellent credentials. The Playboy group asked him to select two or three architectural firms for them to interview and our name was included. The location had already been established. The

La Louisianne Restaurant was to be converted into the Playboy Club according to Hefner's formula for the typical club. The architect to design the club was to be selected by the investors and the Playboy representatives. The major investors were two young men from Chicago. One, Tommy Hughes, owned a large oil and gas distribution company in Chicago, and his partner, Bobby Blum, was a real estate investor in the Chicago area. They flew into New Orleans on a private Playboy jet to interview the three firms, and we were chosen to meet with Hefner at the Playboy Mansion in Chicago.

We were greeted at the door by Mr. Hefner in his usual attire, modified pajamas and a very elaborate smoking jacket. At the front door we were instructed to take off our shoes since the carpet in the entrance to the house was pure white wool. Since he was already in his bedroom slippers, we were expected to follow him on a tour of the mansion in our stocking feet. We then went to visit the Chicago Playboy Club.

The Clubs were supposed to be the personification of a bachelor's pad with a parlor, a lounge, an entertainment room, and vestibules and semi-private areas for dining. The prototype of each room was based upon the Chicago club, and the La Louisianne Restaurant would have to undergo considerable modifications. The lounge was to be luxurious and was to function as a place to enjoy drinking and conversation. There was also an entertainment room where elaborate shows were performed by major artists from Hollywood, New York, and Chicago. The Chicago Playboy Club had these accommodations with the addition of a dormitory where the bunnies from other cities who were rotated from place to place could be housed for a very limited charge or no charge at all. The club had all necessary amenities for the enjoyment of young bachelors, including a sunken swimming pool and a firemen's pole from the upper floors down through the

Arthur Davis, c. 1970.

main floor into the sunken pool. All of these features were extensively publicized in *Playboy* magazine. In New Orleans we were not able to include the swimming pool or the fireman's pole, but we did allow for the Playboy bunnies to live on site if they so desired.

I had brought some preliminary drawings along to give Hefner an impression of what we wanted to do in New Orleans, and he was very well pleased with our efforts. On the strength of the success of the Playboy Club in New Orleans we were commissioned to do clubs in St. Louis, San Francisco, and Los Angeles (see page 115), which were all modifications of the same theme adapted to the specific sites.

The Playboy Clubs thrived for at least two decades, but gradually each one of the clubs closed with the exception of Hefner's mansion in California.

Expansion: New York, London, and Berlin

One of the greatest compliments that an architect can receive is that the client will come back to him for a repeat commission. We were given the opportunity to do seven different IBM buildings in different parts of the country, including Pittsburgh, Burlington, Newark, Mississippi, and Florida. For a large IBM office building complex in Gaithersburg, Pennsylvania (see page 116), we had the only opportunity ever to work on a "design build" where the contractor was the client.

Each of our IBM buildings was unique in one way or another. For the building in downtown Pittsburgh in the Golden Triangle, we experimented with its structural system. On several projects we had built never-before-attempted structural systems, including the Rivergate Convention Center longspan thin slabs; the Superdome tension ring system; the roof structure of the New Orleans Arena suspended entirely on two concrete ribs (although this technique had been success-

Curtis, Rooney, and Davis.

fully used for a number of years in bridges, it had never been employed in a building); and the lift-slab concrete construction in the Louisiana State Penitentiary at Angola. The IBM Pittsburgh complex, however, was perhaps one of the most challenging structural systems which we ever developed— with the assistance of a very creative engineer named John Skilling from Seattle, Washington. (Skilling also worked with us on the roof vault slab designs for the Rivergate Convention Center in New Orleans and the Louisiana National Bank in Baton Rouge.) With his assistance we created the structural system with two exterior ribs and a central core and no interior columns (see page 116). The Pittsburgh building had a special honor. For the only time in our professional life we had one of our buildings pictured on the client's dividend check. Everyone receiving an IBM dividend that year saw our Pittsburgh office building on the check.

Curtis & Davis prospered and grew, so we decided that we could successfully expand our practice into other areas; hence, we established an office in New York City. One of our principle architects, Walter Rooney, became a partner in the

firm and went to New York to take charge. The New York office received more commissions for IBM as well as for the City of New York Department of Education and libraries in Worcester, Massachusetts, and Fort Washington. In fact, the office was doing so well, I purchased a small brownstone on 38th Street in the Murray Hill section of Manhattan and spent a good deal of time commuting between New Orleans and New York over a fifteen-year period.

In the late fifties we also established an office in London in the Carlton Tower Hotel, owned by our client, Hotel Corporation of America. Since we had designed a number of hotels for this chain in the United States and they were expanding into Europe, I felt we should be a part of their growth and expected to do a number of hotels in Europe for this very aggressive hotel chain, still headed by Roger Sonnabend.

Our London office produced a renovation to the Carlton Tower Hotel, a new hotel at Heathrow International Airport, a hotel at St. Andrews in Scotland, and another for Hotel Corporation of America in Hamburg, Germany. This office was, however, mostly a field office which would prove to be useful

Davis with Leon Chatelain (left), president of the Benjamin Franklin Foundation, before boarding a flight to Berlin, to inspect the site of a $15-million hospital designed by Davis in the German city.

when we were designing a health spa and three cultural centers in Saudi Arabia. During these thrilling times, with such a diversified practice both at home and overseas, 99 percent of the travel was my responsibility, and I established and maintained the liaison between New Orleans and New York and London, and eventually Berlin.

While the Royal Orleans was under construction, I was asked to serve on the jury for the Texas Society of Architects' annual Honor Awards competition in Houston. Another juror was Leon Chatelaine, president of the American Institute of Architects, a distinguished gentleman whose own practice had been primarily in restoration or reproduction of historic traditional buildings. Leon was approximately twenty years older than I, but we seemed to be in agreement as to the merits of all of the projects that we reviewed. Although we were together in Houston for only four days, we developed a rapport and an almost instant friendship.

Two weeks later I received a phone call from Mr. Chatelaine asking if I would be interested in designing a new hospital for the Free University in West Berlin, Germany (see pages 117–20). This was indeed a compliment—and quite a surprise to be considered for such an important commission. At this point our office had experience with only three very small Hill-Burton hospitals of twenty-five to fifty beds, and the Berlin Klinikum was to be not only a major hospital, but a medical teaching center as well and the largest commission our firm had received. I was somewhat concerned whether we were qualified and whether I should undertake such a major commitment. I did know that Hugh Stubbins, who had been one of my instructors at Harvard, had just completed an auditorium in Berlin, referred to by the Germans as Congress Hall. Since we were personal friends, I called and asked Hugh what I should do. He encouraged me to accept the commission. After my discussions with Hugh, I called Leon

Chatelaine and told him that I would be honored to be the architect for the medical center.

The architectural program for the medical center was being prepared by Ralph Walker and members of his firm. Mr. Walker was a past president of the American Institute of Architects and a nationally recognized architect whose firm designed many of Bell Telephone Company's buildings throughout the country. The architectural program was eighteen months in preparation.

Completed in early 1959, the program and a detailed list of particulars for the medical center filled two volumes, each approximately one-inch thick. The detailed program contained not only the philosophical approach of the hospital and medical teaching center, but also listed every room, every item of furniture, and every piece of equipment which would be required for this hospital, when finally operational, to be the most modern in Germany.

From 1959 until the dedication in 1968, American and German board members of the Benjamin Franklin Foundation, the client for the hospital, met three to four times per year, and I was expected to give a progress report on the construction. The early meetings were held in a conference room at Hugh Stubbins's Congress Hall. Unfortunately, we never had the benefit of instantaneous translations, so our meetings were very time consuming. The funding for this construction project was to come equally from the American side—using credits already in hand in Germany—and from the German side, as part of reparations for their aggression in the war.

On my many trips to Washington during these early stages I was privileged to spend a good deal of time with Eleanor Dulles (the sister of John Foster Dulles, secretary of state, and of Allen Dulles, director of the CIA). She ran the Berlin desk at the United States Department of State. We agreed that the new hospital should be the finest of its kind not only in Germany but in Europe. As it developed, it was not only the most advanced, but at that time the largest hospital built in Europe since World War II.

These were historic times in Berlin with the blockade of the city, the Berlin airlift, and later on, the construction of the Berlin Wall. The Russians had everyone on edge. The airlift had just been successfully completed, firmly establishing the United States' commitment to stay as a member of the Allied team governing West Berlin—one sector administered by France, one sector administered by Great Britain, and one sector by the United States. The Russians at this time were continually rattling their sabers, making life as unpleasant as possible for the western allies. West Berlin was an isolated island completely surrounded by East German territory and Russian armament. Three ground corridors were available to

A Visit with Pope Pius XII

When my firm designed a number of elementary schools for the archdiocese of New Orleans, we worked very closely with Monsignor Henry C. Bezou, archdiocesan superintendent of schools from 1943 to 1968, in charge of all Catholic elementary schools in the city. We became close friends. When we began the hospital in Berlin, I decided to fly first to Rome on my way to Berlin. When Monsignor Bezou learned that I was about to visit Rome for the first time, he suggested that he might be able to arrange a private audience with the Pope.

The second day after my arrival there was a knock on the door of my hotel room. Before me stood a six-foot-six-inch member of the Swiss Guards in full medieval regalia who presented to me, on a silver tray, a gold-embossed invitation to visit with Pope Pius XII three days hence at the Vatican.

When I arrived at the Vatican, I was ushered through private entrance to a side door into the Pope's chambers. A private visit with the Pope usually includes fifteen to twenty people, and we were all instructed as to how we should greet the Pope. After a fifteen-minute wait, Pope Pius XII entered the room through a draped doorway and made his way to a platform where he had a special throne from which he blessed us and gave us a short talk in Italian, English, and French. He then came down from the podium and visited with each of the group. He knew a good deal about New Orleans. The whole interview was just a few minutes and after, he visited and gave us each a rosary. The visit was a grand experience and one which will stay with me forever.

My Medical Consultant

Dr. Nelson had problems with the German faculty members who were not entirely satisfied with the space allocated for their own private practice. The first and major difference of opinion was that they believed the hospital should have at least 2,000 beds. Since the hospital was projected to have a student body of not more than 600 students, Dr. Nelson felt that anything more than 800 beds would be unwieldy. After a considerable amount of give and take, we arrived at a figure of 1,200 beds as a maximum, which was begrudgingly approved by the Free University medical administrative personnel.

The second issue concerned a philosophy of teaching. German professors traditionally lectured 100 to 200 students in a large amphitheatre with exhibits. Our plans provided direct closed-circuit television from each of the operating rooms with projectors in the two amphitheatres. We also had observation balconies in the major operating rooms. The German professors, however, wished to have at least four to five major amphitheatres. Dr. Nelson and I felt that the two would be ample. We were at somewhat of an impasse, until the Berlin faculty members flew to America to visit Dr. Nelson's institution, Johns Hopkins. Here the American doctors and the German doctors were able to spend time together evaluating American teaching techniques, in which professors worked the wards with small groups of students. The German doctors and administrators agreed to the concept of bedside teaching and two major amphitheatres.

Berlin, one from Munich, one from Frankfort, and one from Hamburg. These routes were controlled by the East Germans, and unpredictably they would stop all traffic to inspect automobiles and trucks, delaying access on each of these three arteries for as long as twelve or even twenty-four hours. The Russians constantly threatened to take over all of Berlin, and we worried whether we could build the hospital under these conditions. The day before I was to leave for Berlin on my first trip, I called Eleanor Dulles and told her of my concerns since the Russians had threatened to close down all transportation, both land and air. To this day I remember Eleanor's reply: "You have nothing to worry about. If there is any problem, we will come get you, even if we have to come in tanks!" That promise did not give me any great feeling of security, but nevertheless I made my first momentous trip into Berlin in the spring of 1959.

After arriving in Berlin, I was directed to select an associate architect from Berlin to work under my direction. After discussions with Berliners, and with advice from Hugh Stubbins, I decided to use Frans Mocken's firm. Mocken spoke excellent English and had worked with Skidmore, Owings, and Merrill on a project in Bonn. Dr. Russell A. Nelson, the retiring president of Johns Hopkins Medical School, had been asked to be the medical consultant representing the United States during the planning and construction of the Berlin Klinikum.

While we were developing the plans for the building, economists were determining the amount of funds available. We were advised that we should plan the hospital to be built in two phases of 600 beds each. With this directive we diligently analyzed the requirements of the program in order to provide sufficient operating rooms and teaching facilities for the 600 beds to operate as a hospital until the second phase could be built. We created a model of the hospital showing the first phase and indicating how the second phase would be attached at a later date. But Mrs. Dulles would have none of this. Since American financial participation was limited, she made her own recommendations to the Berlin Senate and to the proper agencies in Bonn. Mrs. Dulles was a very persuasive person and refused to take no for an answer. The Germans agreed to increase their percentage of participation from 50 percent to approximately 80 percent so that the entire hospital could be built at one time. On September 22, we received word in Washington from Leon Chatelaine: "It appears as though we will be building the entire project in one fell swoop."

Our plans had to be evaluated by the Bau Polici ("building police"), the agency responsible for ensuring that new buildings followed state rules and regulations then in force. Existing law in 1959 required all hospital beds to have a southern exposure. We decided to incorporate a sawtooth façade on a block that had an east-west orientation; because of the splayed windows, each bed did, in fact, have a southern exposure. We were also informed that any room which would be occupied more than four hours a day had to have an outside exposure. This was of course absolutely impossible to achieve in all areas, but in the lower block, we carved out the center section which opened onto interior gardens. The bed blocks floated over the gardens, and all of the rooms in the administration block and most of the rooms in the student classroom areas had outside exposure. These pleasant architectural features were an ingenious way to use some of the obsolete building laws to our advantage, but it was not possible to accommodate all of the old regulations.

The mayor of Berlin was Willy Brandt, who would later become chancellor of Germany. I asked for an appointment to meet with him concerning the design of the new medical center for the Free University, and he received me in his offices the very next morning. He was not only a dynamic leader, but also a very understanding and compassionate man. I explained to him the dilemma that we were facing because of the regulations of the Bau Polici, reiterating to him that this hospital should be the most modern, the most exciting, and the most efficient hospital in Europe, that we could not compromise with pre-Hitler building regulations. He was very sympathetic and understood our problem.

"Leave this to me," he said. "I would like to have you as my guest for a small reception tomorrow evening, and you will be at my quarters at six o'clock." The next evening he asked me to stand with him in a receiving line for this occasion. In Germany, unlike in America, the guests arrive promptly at the appointed hour according to their invitations. Officials from the Bau Polici were invited as well as professors, doctors, and members of the staff of the medical center. After greeting everyone and being introduced to each one individually by the mayor of West Berlin, we had a very pleasant cocktail party with hors d'oeuvres, soft drinks, and wine. Nothing was discussed at the party concerning our problems with the hospital design. A little after seven o'clock the party was over, and I thanked Mayor Brandt for affording me this opportunity to meet all of these people. He said that it was his pleasure and that I should not worry about regulatory restraints, that I should just create the most modern, economical, and efficient hospital possible. From that day forward we had no problem with the Bau Polici.

Those were exciting times in Berlin, and none of us suspected that overnight the city would be divided in two. On August 13, 1961, the Russians and East Germans began erecting the infamous Berlin Wall. It had a direct effect on our hospital construction since approximately 50 percent of our workmen commuted from East Berlin every day, and they were completely cut off. To aggravate the situation even more, almost all of our cement supply, so vitally needed for

Meeting Robert Kennedy in Berlin

Many dignitaries come to Berlin, most of them visiting the Klinikum site, and I was present when President John F. Kennedy gave his "Ich bin ein Berliner" speech at the infamous Wall. As I listened to him in Berlin, I remembered an earlier time, standing in front of the speaker's platform in the snow in Washington when Kennedy gave his inaugural address during which he said, "Ask not what your country can do for you; ask what you can do for your country." During the Cuban missile crisis, we were all concerned that we were on the verge of another war. I recommended that Val Dansereau, our resident architect on the site, leave Berlin, because if anything were to happen in Cuba, Berlin would probably have been overrun by Russians on the same day.

In February 1962, Attorney General Bobby Kennedy visited Berlin, and I was invited to a reception in his honor at the Schlotenberg Schloss, a magnificent castle located in the suburbs of Berlin. Bobby Kennedy's press secretary, Edward Guthman, a newspaperman from Seattle, was the brother of a close personal friend in New Orleans. He arranged for me to meet with the attorney general the afternoon before the gala. The meeting was held in one of the spacious offices of the palace, decorated with magnificent traditional furniture, obviously imported from France—inlaid wood with gold accents.

When I arrived, Bobby Kennedy greeted me in a friendly, informal way—his feet were up on this beautiful desk, and he was wearing sneakers. We talked about Berlin and his brother's strong commitment to protecting the people of West Berlin. He asked me to describe the Klinikum and appeared to have a genuine interest in what we were building. He was very encouraging.

The evening festivities were indeed a very gala affair—the entire castle was lit by candles, and this created a wonderful illusion with the beautiful gilded moldings in the grand ballrooms and the ladies in their finest evening dresses. I would later discover that the lighting of candles is a traditional custom for sad occasions as well as happy events. Some time later, Val, our architect in Berlin, gave a moving description to me of the ceremonial lighting of candles in Berlin to mourn the assassination of President Kennedy.

this massive building, came by barges on the Teltow Canal, which also was cut off by the Wall. We found other sources for the cement, and the contractors brought in outside labor, many not as efficient as the German workers that were lost. But they did the job, and we were able to finish the hospital in spite of the Wall.

The conceptual design and all schematics for the hospital were developed in New Orleans, as were most of the presentation drawings. Design development and working drawings were all produced in Berlin in Frans Mockin's office. In order to control our designs as the working drawings and construction progressed, we set up a field office in Berlin with one of our senior architects continually on the site. As it developed, we had a tour of duty of approximately two years for each of our architects. They did not consider this a great hardship but more of an exciting adventure.

Postwar Berlin was an interesting place with much new construction under way. Large historic hotels, such as the Kempinsky, were available for visitors, and Hilton had just completed a highrise, 250-room hotel complex nearby. But the Hotel AmZoo was the favorite of most of our people coming to Berlin to work on the Klinikum. It had no more than thirty rooms and was conveniently located on the Kuferstendam adjacent to all of best restaurants, shops, and night life. Since it was very small, the guests considered it more of a guest house than a conventional hotel. Most of the architects from abroad stayed at the AmZoo, and it became my home away from home. One delightful evening I had the privilege to share a late supper with Walter Gropius and Mies Van der Rohe at our hotel. It was a little difficult for me since these two distinguished gentlemen spoke German throughout the evening, but it was an opportunity for me to try to improve my conversational German. During these evenings together, Dr. Gropius and I reminisced over our times together at Har-

vard, and Mies presented his views on new buildings under construction in Berlin, especially, his pure Glass Box museum placed on a huge solid windowless base four stories high.

Since I spent a good deal of time in Berlin commuting from our New York and New Orleans offices, after a time I decided that it might be more convenient to have a permanent flat where I could keep clothes, files, and other material, rather than carrying them back and forth on airplanes. In 1964 I met and became friends with developer Carl Heinz Pepper, a very aggressive entrepreneur who had built a number of office and apartment complexes in Berlin. Mr. Pepper was building an apartment complex and major shopping center on Budapestestrasser at the termination of the Kuferstendam, and he proposed that if we would design the penthouses on the top of his apartment complex, he would permit me to have the use of one for a limited time at a very reasonable rent. We designed four magnificent penthouses overlooking the entire city of Berlin. In lieu of his having to pay us an architectural fee, for two years I enjoyed one of the penthouses for a nominal fee. When I moved out, he quadrupled the rent.

The years passed and the work progressed at an ever-increasing pace, and we were all enthusiastically looking forward to the grand opening. The dedication ceremonies for the Klinikum were held in the large auditorium of the Congress Hall, since there were no spaces in the Klinikum large enough to accommodate all of the visitors, dignitaries, and press. The Berlin Symphony Orchestra gave a concert. There were speeches by Leon Chatelaine; Eleanor Dulles, representing the State Department; Senator Henry Cabot Lodge; and members of the Berlin Senate. The architects were recognized, and I was able to limp through a speech, half of which was in German.

Crossing the Berlin Wall

I had no love for the Russian or the East German governments. That might have been one of the reasons I decided to smuggle some East Germans to freedom, an experience which I have never divulged until now.

When the Wall was built, not only were workers separated from their jobs; family members were also tragically separated from each other. Many attempted to cross from East to West, but few were successful. Frequently they were killed in the attempt. Although I detested the situation, I was not directly involved until some of my German friends began speaking of the many people who wanted to cross over to the West. Werner Duttman—one of Berlin's most talented architects and a dear friend—and I thought we might have a solution to this problem.

At that time I had a rather dilapidated model 190 Mercedes that I kept in Berlin as a convenience. When I was not in Berlin, other members of my staff used the car. Werner Duttman and I discovered the back seat could be removed and hinged, creating a good-sized pocket. Border guards at Checkpoint Charlie usually looked in the trunk and inside the car, and with their mirrors on wheels, looked under the car and under the hood by the motor. But beneath the back seat was a foolproof hiding spot.

I traveled to East Berlin on many occasions and discovered that if I approached the checkpoint with a diplomat from a neutral country in the car, we usually would be waved through without any inspection whatsoever.

After the back seat of the Mercedes was rigged to receive visitors, I would tell Werner Duttman when I was going over to East Berlin, where I would be parking the car, how long I would be there, and when I would return. I never knew to whom this information was given. When I drove to East Berlin, I parked the Mercedes in a designated location and after dinner or the ballet, I drove the car back through Checkpoint Charlie—in some instances with no inspection, and other times, a very thorough one. Back in the West, I would park the car in a specific location and leave it for the night. I had these rendezvous ten or twelve times, and each time everything went smoothly. I never saw any of the people I ferried across the checkpoint, but I am told that between twelve and fourteen people, either friends or relatives of some of our associates, were reunited with their loved ones because of the old, beat-up 190 Mercedes.

The hospital was reviewed in a number of architectural and hospital supply magazines, both in Germany and abroad. Many of the features of the design were used in a new medical complex in Japan. Medical journals featured different aspects of the design, including the food service system, the operating room suites with the communication-assisted teaching aides, including the observation mezzanine and the closed circuit television to the student amphitheatres.

The Klinikum has been recognized in a number of ways. On November 18, 1966, a stamp with an image of the new medical center was issued in Berlin; so, along with the postage stamp of the U.S.S. *Missouri*, my designs have been placed on postage stamps in two different countries. In 1994 the hospital complex was renamed Universitatsklinkum Benjamin Franklin to honor the role of the Benjamin Franklin Foundation in the establishment of this wonderful facility in postwar Berlin.

The Politics of Architecture in New Orleans: The New Orleans Public Library and the Missing Alferez Statue

I very much enjoy designing buildings which provide spiritual and intellectual inspiration. The first library for which we were commissioned was the main branch of the New Orleans Public Library in 1955. Our design approach was somewhat radical for a library and the effort to have it accepted was a difficult one. Thankfully we had the support of the new director of the New Orleans library system, Mr. John Hall Jacobs, who gave us the inspiration, incentive, and support necessary to accomplish this revolution. Previously all libraries in New Orleans turned their backs on the environment and gave the impression of a cloistered, quiet area for study and meditation. At that time the main branch was housed in a three-story masonry structure which was massive, depress-

ing, and in no way conducive to enticing the public to come in to enjoy the benefits of learning through the use of books and periodicals. Mr. Jacobs's concept was to replace this obsolete, monolithic masonry structure with a light and airy building that would be an obvious invitation to the community to come and enjoy.

We agreed that the library should be more in the spirit of a spacious department store for books where everything might be visible from all locations in the building (see pages 121–23). In other words, if one were browsing in the Louisiana section, one would also be aware of other activities in the area devoted to science or technology or even the children's department. We built a model of the proposed glass-box building and presented it to the library board with the support of Mr. Jacobs. We had recommended that the aluminum screen, the major architectural feature of the building, be constructed of gold anodized aluminum, which would reflect the sun's ray and give the building sparkle while providing a certain elegance to a very simple but graceful design. The design was approved by the library board.

The library board presented the proposed scheme to the mayor, in what we thought was a formality, and we expected him to be very pleased. The mayor at that time, DeLesseps S. Morrison, was a young, dynamic leader who became the first reform mayor of the city in more than a generation. He immediately reacted against the idea of a gold anodized sun screen for the building. He was not opposed to a sun screen or to the design, but he did not want the community to feel that his administration would be building "gold-plated" structures. He demanded that the aluminum screen be modified in color if not in concept. This was a terribly disappointing development, but we were forced to specify naturally colored aluminum in lieu of the gold anodized. The building lost a great deal because of this modification, but it still stands and works very well as a focal point of the city hall complex. The special sun screen design of anodized aluminum was perhaps the most delicate of all the sun screens employed in any of our structures.

For additional protection against direct sunlight, we planted a row of magnolia trees. Now that the trees have grown, the lower branches have been trimmed so that the view through the glass wall into the library proper is not obstructed, and the beauty of these mature handsome magnolia trees completes the original concept of the library complex as a whole.

Our decision to keep the glass box above grade and have all of the closed stacks below involved a few technical problems. Since the water table in New Orleans was six to eight feet below the surface, the stack area needed to be constructed as a watertight box, and in fact, the basement was designed similar to a floating vessel. The pilings to support the building were anchored to the concrete base in order to offset the upward thrust caused by the high water table. Until the super structure over the base—namely the three floors above the ground—was constructed, the pilings literally held the building down against the negative water pressure until the weight of the upper floors counterbalanced the force of the water pressure. The structure would then be stable.

Since a great percentage of the books were below the water table, the area allocated to closed stacks had no openings to the exterior. The Sewerage and Water Board of New Orleans furnished us with information about potential flood levels in that area of the city, and access to the stacks was in all instances above the maximum projected flood level elevation. As additional insurance we installed sump pumps in the double basement, and to this day there has never been any water seepage in the basement. The books stored be-

low grade happily are all dry, well preserved, and protected against the elements, especially flooding.

To the best of my knowledge, we set a new direction for public libraries by enticing the people into the building to see and feel and smell the books, rather than fostering the idea that these were sacred halls not to be used by the general public. We recognized that this was not a research library but a library where the citizens of New Orleans could browse, select books, and be inspired to return time and again to enjoy the many different vistas and interesting spaces which the library had to offer. I know of no other libraries at the time which were conceived with the philosophy of an open "department store" concept. Our firm built three other libraries, one in Worcester, Massachusetts; one in Port Washington, New York; and one in Patterson, New Jersey. These were smaller libraries but were the main public branches in their respective cities. In each instance we expanded on this same conception of the open plan.

It is rather difficult to design public buildings with federal, state, or city funding without having to justify the designs to the political "Powers That Be," and in my career I have dealt with some fascinating politicians. As I have described, Mayor Chep Morrison changed the final visual appearance of the New Orleans Public Library for purely political reasons, and this was not to be the last time this occurred. I had an additional confrontation with Mayor Morrison concerning a piece of sculpture for a district courthouse and jail in the first precinct in New Orleans.

We designed a relatively modest precinct building, with a jail and small municipal court for minor offenses, for a site on North Rampart Street, the northern boundary of the French Quarter. The front wall of the police facility was conceived as a solid marble slab with no need for windows. The cell block

Davis (center), inspecting the site of the Jewish Community Center, New Orleans, with building committee chair Lewis Sizeler (right).

and the courtroom windows were to be located in the rear and on the side elevations. We selected Enrique Alferez, a very distinguished Mexican sculptor whose studio and workshops were in New Orleans, to create pieces of sculpture for the front elevation of our building. He had created art pieces for the Lakefront Airport and additional works in City Park, all under the auspices of WPA. After consultation with Mr. Alferez, we decided that a piece emphasizing the importance of the family might be an appropriate theme, and he agreed to develop a design comprising a man, a woman, and a child representing the importance of the family unit. The composition was perfect for the location on the white marble slab façade facing North Rampart Street. Mr. Alferez completed the piece and arranged to have it mounted in place. The sculpture was unveiled by the mayor in a very low-key ceremony at the dedication of the new precinct station. The statue was an exceptionally fine sculpture, very handsome and beautifully executed, and everyone seemed to approve.

The day after the statue was unveiled, we received a call from Mayor Morrison asking us to come immediately to City Hall for a meeting. Much to our surprise, he informed us that he had received a complaint from the members of a church congregation. Our Lady of Guadalupe Chapel International Shrine of St. Jude, located a block from the precinct station, strongly objected to the sculpture because all three figures were presented in the nude—and the male figure which dominated the group had exposed genitals which could be viewed from the street. Mayor Morrison demanded that we immediately instruct the sculptor to add a fig leaf to the piece. This would appease all parties concerned. When we passed this request on to Enrique Alferez, he vehemently opposed this suggestion and refused to add the fig leaf. Although we did not think the change was necessary, we did everything in our power, in order to save his piece, to entice the sculptor to bring modesty to the family group. When he absolutely refused to do so, we reported back to the mayor, and the mayor said either the fig leaf or no sculpture. The next day when we arrived at the site, the statue had been covered in burlap, and the following day it was removed from the building. We were told to replace it with something less controversial. Kaiser Aluminum offered to donate an aluminum map of North and South America which in no way fit the space, but was immediately approved by Mayor Morrison and installed within a month. To this day we have no idea where the Alferez statue is. In general our relationship with Mayor Morrison was always friendly, since we strongly endorsed his reform policies and his desires to make the city administration more responsive to the needs of the people. He was a first-rate mayor and a good politician; however, in these two instances he might have been practicing good politics, but he was insensitive to protecting the integrity of the arts.

From the Caribbean to the North Sea: Aruba and Scotland

The island of Aruba has a flat, rather uninteresting natural terrain, but its ample white-sand beaches and its location between Venezuela and Florida has made it a popular

Voodoo in Haiti

Although Haiti is almost exclusively Catholic, voodoo is intricately woven into the people's beliefs and does not conflict with their Christianity. The same seems to be true with voodoo as it is practiced in New Orleans. I made contact with a local guide who became my friend and mentor. Jean-Paul took me to see the voodoo ceremonies that were staged weekly for the tourists, complete with drum beating, dancing on fire, sacrificing of roosters, and other rituals. But I wanted to see more. On the way home from one of these presentations, I told Jean-Paul I was interested in voodoo beyond what was displayed for tourists, and I explained to him about my own experiences with voodoo in New Orleans. I said I had carried a charm with me through my navy tour of duty in the Pacific during World War II. He stopped the car, turned, looked at me in the eye, and said, "Are you really a believer?"

I considered Jean-Paul's question and replied. "To the extent that I understand what is involved in voodoo, I am a believer."

"Well in that case, I will take you tomorrow night to a place where you will have an opportunity to experience firsthand how voodoo can be useful to you in your future life."

Needless to say, I was intrigued.

The next day, we drove out of Port au Prince up into the hills toward the southwest. After about an hour, we finally arrived at a pasture where burros were grazing and chickens and pigs roamed about. At the far end of the clearing stood a shed. In this shelter were rows of cots occupied by patients of the local witch doctor.

I received a cursory review of the hospital and a tour through the rows of cots with seated men, women, and children who appeared to be waiting for treatment from the witch doctor, or "hougon." After a short time, I was greeted by the hougon himself. His most unusual feature was that he appeared to be continually smiling. Upon closer observation, it was clear that his upper lip was missing, and in fact, he was very serious and not grinning at all. He had a sparkle in his eye that indicated he understood everything that was going on and was prepared to deal with me on his own terms.

Using Jean-Paul as interpreter, he led me to a small pristine white stucco building with a green door and three black wooden steps leading to a single room. I was shocked by the scene that greeted me and tried hard to take it all in and not miss any details. Inside, the space was lit only by candles, and the walls were painted in wonderful floral designs. Opposite the entry door was a small altar with a series of shelves gradually receding toward the ceiling. On the altar were the implements of the hougon's trade, including a deck of cards, which showed years of heavy use, and small charms, bells, whistles, and gongs intended to conjure up good spirits to assist him in his evaluation of my fortune. Two small stools were placed in front of the altar—he occupied one and indicated that I should take the second.

The hougon then proceeded to shuffle the cards, bending them almost in two and laying them out on the small shelf which Jean-Paul referred to as his altar. The fortune telling took approximately twenty minutes, and I learned a great deal about future activities and potential for success in my profession as well as my personal life. I must admit in all candor that almost all of the predictions—which I remember somewhat vaguely after these many years—were exceedingly accurate.

When he completed his analysis, he returned the deck to the altar shelf and thanked me for my close attention, and I thanked him for his very intriguing presentation. All this was done in French and Creole patois, which required a good deal of translation by Jean-Paul. As I rose to leave the inner chamber, the hougon asked me whether I would be interested in having a wish granted through another ceremony. He informed me through Jean-Paul that it was a rather expensive ceremony—it would cost me $100. Jean-Paul translated this and assured me that it would be worth the money. I authorized the hougon to proceed with the necessary preparations to grant me a wish. I had no idea how this would affect my future life or, more immediately, what the ceremony would involve.

We were then led out to another white stucco bungalow adjoining the first one. This one had a bright red door. It was also lit inside exclusively by candles, and the walls were again covered with murals, but these depictions were more sinister. Where the first cottage was tranquil, this one felt full of evil. There was the same shelf below the murals with the candles placed every two feet around the room, but in the two corners adjacent to the entry door, two large, live black roosters sat placidly between the flames of the candles.

A small black casket rested on a high shelf near the ceiling, surrounded by small figures which we in Louisiana call voodoo ceremonial dolls, or fetishes. On the wall opposite the entrance there was an altar as well, but quite different in appearance from the other. Over the altar, suspended by a heavy-link steel chain, a large rock hung in space.

The hougon asked me to sit in front of the altar. He then removed a series of rattles and bells from the lower shelf and addressed me with chants and Creole songs in a slow dirge tempo. After circling my stool seven times repeating the chants, he put back the rattles and bells and requested that I removed my shoes and stockings. He then opened a trap door on the floor at the opposite end of the room from the entrance. I hesitated, but felt that at this point I was committed. So I followed the hougon down the damp and slippery stone steps to the cellar below. In the center of the room a single large candle illuminated the entire space. Here again black live roosters were stationed in the four corners of the basement.

Cantilevered off the wall opposite the steps was a large black coffin draped with a white sheet. It appeared to be floating in space but actually was supported by metal brackets anchored to the masonry wall. The hougon directed me to climb into the coffin and cross my hands over my chest and I dutifully obeyed. At this moment he shouted to a young assistant, who immediately descended the stairs holding a live pigeon which he handed to the hougon. The boy then stood next to the casket holding a large pewter dish. With a great deal of ceremony, the hougon placed the bird, still holding it firmly in his grip, on my forehead and asked me to think of my wish. Then he placed the bird on my chest and once again asked me to think of my wish. He went on down my entire body three times, in each case requiring that I concentrate on my wish as strongly as possible. He then held the pigeon over the pewter dish and unceremoniously twisted the bird's head off from its body, turned the bird upside down, and drained its blood into the bowl. He then took the bowl from the young boy, gave him the pigeon, and asked me to proceed with him to the chamber above.

The hougon placed my stool in the center of the room and asked me to hold the dish on my lap. He then stirred herbs, corn-meal, seaweed, grass, and grains of corn into the pigeon blood with a whisk and walked around me seven times, throwing part of the solution from the whisk up toward the ceiling, some of it falling onto my head and shoulders. Each time he circled me he reminded me to think of my wish while he continued to spray me with the solution from the bowl. He then said that he would be leaving the room; I should strip down and bathe myself in the remaining solution. When I had completed this ritual, I was to summon him with three knocks on the red door. I must confess I

did not remove all of my clothing but gently applied a portion of the solution to my forehead, my wrists, my ankles, and the back of my neck.

When he returned, he removed a large stone from the altar and asked me to hold it in my hands while I thought of my wish. He then bathed the rock in the pigeon-blood concoction, set one white candle in the center of the rock, lit it, and asked me to hold the rock, continually thinking of my wish. He took the candle and traversed me three times singing beautiful chants. After the third circle he relieved me of the stone, placed it on the altar, and gently rubbed the stone with a clean white handkerchief. He wrapped the candle in the handkerchief and poured the remainder of the solution from the dish into a small vial which he handed to me. He advised me that when I returned home, if I would spray the front step with this solution, it would protect my house from any future evil spirits. I should use the solution sparingly and keep it locked away in a safe place. The candle and handkerchief should be also cherished since they would protect me, grant me continued prosperity, and keep me in a constant state of well being. He said that I need not worry, that my wish would be fulfilled and that I should now return to the United States with the knowledge that I would be under his protection with nothing to fear.

Back in New Orleans I faithfully sprinkled the potion on the front step of my Bourbon Street house, and we never were disturbed by the ghosts my children insisted were in the attic.

resort. In the early 1970s, we were commissioned to design the Aruba Concordia Hotel for a Venezuelan banking group (see page 124). The banks in Venezuela are very adventurous and creative, not nearly as conservative as the American banks. The young owners of one of the largest banks in Caracas visited New Orleans and fell in love with the feel of the city—the food, the entertainment, the jazz. They stayed at the Royal Sonesta, the hotel we designed on Bourbon Street, and decided that we should be the architects for their hotel on Aruba. I visited the site, a barren beach with a number of undistinguished, small hotels adjacent to our location, and I was convinced that here was an opportunity to design an exciting structure that would relate to the crystal blue Caribbean waters and the pristine, sugary beaches. The resulting structure was somewhat in the spirit of a Vascerelli three-dimensional painting. A casino at the beach level kept the hotel in the black. The beaches, swimming pools, and landscaping to the south completed the holiday ambiance. It was by far the most attractive tourist hotel on Aruba.

We later designed a hotel overlooking the Charles River in Cambridge, Massachusetts, with the same problems of shielding the view of a depressed area to the north. There, all of the rooms face the Charles River to the south, blocking out the unacceptable rear views. We also used this design feature on a hotel in Detroit, Michigan.

There were curious aspects of dealing with the young, carefree Venezuelan bankers. On all occasions we documented our proposals in writing, including our potential contract and our description of the building with our cost estimates and all the related correspondence. But strangely enough, our clients in Venezuela never responded in writing. This made us exceedingly nervous and forced us to fly to Aruba frequently to meet with them in person. We even had to go personally to Caracas monthly to pick up our payments.

With all of the accompanying fellowship and socializing in Venezuela during these days of their oil boom, our Venezuelan clients also became good friends.

In 1972 I stopped off in Haiti on my way to collect our fees in Caracas. Haiti was very intriguing to me: the people friendly to strangers, and I was fascinated by their art. The primitive yet sophisticated depictions of native life on the island of Haiti and the artistic interpretations of their religious beliefs created dramatic and highly sensitive paintings. Their sculpture using sheet metal was very powerful. I visited Haiti en route to Venezuela on a number of occasions and collected quite a few paintings as well as pieces of sculpture. I stayed at the Grand Hotel Olafson, a wonderful, Victorian, wood-frame structure with gingerbread ornamentation and large, high-ceilinged guest rooms with ceiling fans and white wicker furniture. It was everything that a tropical island hotel should be and apparently was the most popular spot for visiting celebrities who wanted to get away from the conventional tourist hotels. Ernest Hemingway spent a great deal of time in the Grand Hotel Olafson, as did other authors, actors and other celebrities.

In the early 1970s, there was no true prosperity in Haiti, but the people seemed comfortable, and many of them were able to devote time toward artistic endeavors. Local artists displayed their products in a number of small art galleries, and I was among many visitors to the island who became avid collectors of Haitian art.

Fate continued to play a part in my life in unusual ways. Mr. Phillip Shirley, chairman of the board of British Railways, was responsible for the operation of all British Railway's hotels throughout England and Scotland, including major hotels in almost every important city where British Railways had a terminal. When he visited New Orleans, he stayed at the Royal Orleans Hotel and was impressed with the ambiance, decor, and the spaciousness of the public areas, and the effectiveness of the hotel as a part of the urban scene. Mr. Shirley was so enamored with our hotel he searched us out and asked us whether we would like to design a hotel for British Railways in Scotland in the town of St. Andrews. We told him we would be delighted.

Building a hotel on sacred ground—facing the St. Andrews golf course, the fountainhead of golf—was an awesome responsibility for us. I never played a single hole on the St. Andrews course to the consternation of many of my golfing friends, but I did walk the course a number of times. Since our site was a plot of land abutting the historic course, the course had to be considered an integral part of our design criteria.

Every hole on the original golf course was named either for the hazards or a famous golfer, and the seventeenth hole, directly adjacent to our site, was referred to as "The Sheds." The site itself was an old goods yard—the American translation would be a warehouse—with railroad spurs attached to structures long since abandoned. Part of an ancillary shed extended out to the edge of the seventeenth hole fairway, creating a dogleg hazard which required driving either over the shed or around it. We were instructed that we could not demolish The Sheds because they were historically important to the old course. This was very disconcerting since The Sheds were ramshackled old frame structures with no aesthetic significance whatsoever. We decided to measure the exact silhouette of The Sheds and construct a wing of the proposed new hotel using The Sheds configuration as a part of a solarium overlooking the seventeenth hole. Since it was apparent that many golfers attempting to drive over The Sheds actually hit the structure, we were obliged to design the walls either of solid masonry or timber; where we included glass, we were careful to incorporate shatter-proof,

temperate double-thickness glazing. This was an acceptable addition to the hotel and preserved the necessary obstacle to the dogleg of the seventeenth hole.

We decided that the public areas should be on the roof since the vistas over the golf course and out toward the sea were quite dramatic; therefore with the exception of a small reception area at the ground level, all of the lobbies, registration area, dining rooms, and public spaces were on the upper level.

This was a relatively small hotel. In the first phase our instructions were to design a hotel of ninety rooms. This would not be a terribly efficient hotel since the amount of public space needed for ninety rooms would be almost the same as that required for a hotel of twice that size; however, the British Railways was adamant that they wished to build only ninety rooms until the hotel proved to be a success. Since the hotel faced the original golf course, the name selected was the Old Course Hotel, and it is still known by that name to this day. It was also referred to as "the upside down hotel," since the public areas were on the upper level instead of on the ground floor.

The Old Course Hotel, with the approval of Royal and Ancient Golf Club, was built as designed and was exceedingly well received by the public (see page 125). One of the architects from our firm, Fritz Suchke, who was working in our London office at the time, worked with the interiors group of British Railways who refurbished the rooms and public areas of the British Railways hotels. This staff, working with Fritz, selected furnishings and fixtures from Scottish sources. The furniture was either of Scottish manufacture or of our design built in Scotland by Scottish craftsmen. The fabrics in almost all instances were woven in Scotland out of Scottish wools and of designs which were universally accepted as historically Scottish in origin. Beautiful, woven upholstery

Davis, Krewe of Rex parade, 1975.

incorporated the colors of Scottish plaids, and the interiors were warm, friendly, and conducive to good fellowship in a climate which was harsh and in many instances forbidding.

A few years later, the British Railway group doubled the size of the hotel just as we had anticipated; however, Phillip Shirley was no longer the acting chairman and the Powers That Be selected another architect from Scotland to do the additions—which I must say were very much in sympathy with the original design.

The Rivergate

In the 1950s, business and civic leaders in New Orleans conceived the idea of a major exhibition facility to help promote the city as a center for world trade. The project, spearheaded by the International House, the International Trade Mart, and later the Chamber of Commerce, received the approval of Mayor Morrison and the city administration. To be built on a six-block site bounded by Canal, Poydras, South Peters

Streets, and Convention Center Boulevard, the facility would feature offices, meeting rooms, concession facilities, and a large exhibit hall which could accommodate such activities as international trade shows, large banquets, carnival balls, and other major events.

The New Orleans Dock Board, composed of prominent local businessmen and headed by director, Jim Amoss, selected the firm of Curtis & Davis to design the facility. Rivergate, the Port of New Orleans Exhibition Center, was a significant monument in the city of New Orleans (see pages 126–27). Intended to be an exhibition hall, it was a graceful and romantic structure using reinforced concrete in a way that was light and delicate. We spanned 253 feet with slabs that were only 5½ inches thick. Although the walls of the building itself were hammered reinforced concrete, the contrast between the enclosure and the floating roof was unique. Not only was that great swooping roof beautiful; it also allowed for a major porte-cochere and canopy for people arriving and departing the exhibitions that were held in the Rivergate during its heyday. The great open interior spaces could be divided in almost any way.

In 1969, the year after it was completed, the Rivergate won the Honor Award from the Louisiana Architects Association, a chapter of the American Institute of Architects. It was written about in major national and international architectural and construction publications. Architects and engineers from around the world came to study the creative design and the complex construction. In 1994, the American Institute of Architects New Orleans gave it a Special Honor Award. There is no question that the Rivergate was a significant monument in the city of New Orleans.

Unfortunately, in the early 1990s, city officials, looking to cash in on newly revived gambling revenue, decided to replace the Rivergate with a dockside casino. Friends of Rivergate, a group of concerned citizens organized to oppose the destruction of the building, tried unsuccessfully to save it by nominating it for the National Register of Historic Places. The reasoning of the Louisiana State Historic Preservation Office not to process the nomination stated that there was "no consent in writing by the owner [City of New Orleans]" and in their "professional opinion the building did not appear to meet National Register criteria." The Keeper of the National Register concurred with the decision of the Louisiana State Historic Preservation Office.

In 1995, the Rivergate was demolished. New Orleans, a city famous for the preservation of its distinctive culture, traditions, music, history, and architecture, lost a national treasure.

Curtis & Davis always tried to design buildings with lasting qualities using materials that have permanency. Today many buildings being built have a life expectancy of twenty to thirty years. Our throw-away society has come to expect that in that space of time a building will have outgrown its useful-ness and should be torn down. That's a dangerous mind-set that permits buildings to be destroyed with no regard to the significance of the long history of the architecture community.

Louisiana Superdome

The Louisiana Superdome is a New Orleans icon, impacting much more than just the city's skyline. When it opened in 1975, it was an economic shot in the arm for New Orleans and a catalyst for downtown development. It is emblematic of the city's tourism and entertainment industries, the main drivers of the economy, even today (see pages 128–29).

The Dome was the largest commission Curtis & Davis had ever landed, perhaps with the exception of the Berlin Medical Center. David Dixon, businessman and sports executive, dreamed of having an enclosed stadium in Louisiana to rival the Houston Astrodome. The Astrodome, the first ballpark in the world to have a roof, was built in 1966 for approximately $35 million and seated about 55,000 fans. Dixon convinced Governor John McKeithen to push for the arena.

To select the architects for this very important project, McKeithen asked the deans of the architecture schools at Louisiana universities to recommend firms, and they presented him with two firms: Curtis & Davis and the prestigious firm of Skidmore, Owings, and Merrill of New York. McKeithen suggested we meet with SOM and work out a way to jointly take on the responsibility for designing the Louisiana Superdome. A series of conferences with the New York firm were entirely unsatisfactory. SOM wanted us to be their local junior associates and assist with supervision, but they planned to execute the actual creative designs in New York. We couldn't live with that, and we informed the governor that he would have to choose between SOM and Curtis & Davis. This was risky. We were being pitted against one of the largest firms in the country. We wanted to be involved in this major project, but we had to participate at least on equal terms. Happily, on August 11, 1970, we were selected as the lead architects. The governor added two other Louisiana architectural firms—Silverstein, Matherson, Bergman and Norman, Nolan, and Nolan—but he designated us as the chief designers.

The state legislature approved the building of an arena comparable to the Houston Astrodome, with an authorized budget of approximately $35 million. McKeithen, however, had bigger ideas. New Orleans was already hosting sold-out events, including the Superbowl, the Sugar Bowl, and Tulane-LSU football games, in the 80,000-seat Tulane Stadium. McKeithen believed that this should be the minimum capacity for the Dome. Moreover, he wanted more elaborate amenities than those at the Astrodome. And since the building would be an important anchor to the Central Business District, he believed that it should be an architecturally significant structure. Finally, he wanted parking for 5,000 cars within the building.

We were delighted to design a bigger and better stadium than the Astrodome, but the governor's ideas would cost considerably more than the $35 million which had been authorized by the legislature. He directed us to proceed and to leave the politics and the funding to him. With a great deal of trepidation, we designed the larger stadium. Once the conceptual designs and preliminary working drawings were completed, permitting us to accurately ascertain the costs, we advised Governor McKeithen that the structure he envisioned would cost approximately $121 million—and that was just for "bricks and mortar." At this point, we assumed the project was doomed and the Superdome would never become a reality.

We underestimated McKeithen. He presented the new budget to the legislature, who approved the issuing of bonds to build the Louisiana Superdome as we had conceived it. With all fees, land costs, and financing, the final price tag of the project was $156 million.

At C&D, all commissions were assigned to either Curtis or me as the partner-in-charge, the person who would be responsible for deciding who would work on the project and how it would be handled. For the Superdome, Curtis was the lead architect and carried out his duties in an exemplary fashion.

There were many dramatic moments in the construction of the Dome, each one watched nervously by the public. Early on, a Tulane University structural engineer told the media that he did not believe the building would be safe. To allay fears, we had to demonstrate, once again, the safety of the design to the commission overseeing the construction. The Superdome was unique. Since no one had ever before attempted a building exactly like it, we were committed to ensuring the soundness of the structure. As it turned out, when the Dome was finished, there was absolutely no settlement, and today, more than thirty years later, the building is as sturdy as the day it was completed.

Because the conceived dome was so much larger than the Astrodome, we had to invent a new way to create and support the enormous roof. The building was to be as large as the Coliseum in Rome, and the roof, spanning almost ten acres, would be the largest in the country. We had to solve the problem of horizontal thrust, the tendency of an arched roof to push outwards. Normally, such a design would require buttresses similar to those on the gothic cathedrals of Europe. But our engineers came up with the idea of a tension ring that went all the way around the building like a belt (see page 128).

Once the roof was in place, we faced an unforeseen problem. During construction, hundreds of pigeons flew in and out of the building. The birds were now trapped, and as they soared around the largest domed building in the world, they seemed in no hurry to leave their $150-million home. The story was widely covered by the media, and for weeks amused citizens all over Louisiana submitted their solutions to the problem. Fortunately pigeons were not within our area of responsibility, and we proceeded with matters of design and construction while others shooed the birds. Other problems concerned workmen stealing pieces of the exterior coating of the roof as souvenirs and our neighbors in the nearby public housing complex using the roof for target practice. Periodically, we had to repair the patches.

Although it has been likened to a spaceship, the Dome is no doubt beautiful, and truly enhances and defines the New Orleans skyline. Because our design philosophy demanded functionality over aesthetics, the elegant lip along the connection between the roof and the vertical walls is actually a gutter. Twelve feet deep, it collects and controls rainwater as it rolls off the roof. If it were not there, downtown New Orleans could be flooded by every hard rain.

Since 80,000 seats were a very large order, the competition for the selection of the manufacturer and installer was intense, and even political. We looked into international designs and found that the Italians had a beautiful seat that was very economical and efficient, easy to erect and easy to replace. However, the American manufacturers objected. We finally agreed upon an American design that was not quite as efficient as the Italian one but was politically acceptable.

At that time seating in large sports arenas was all one color. We believed that an innovative color-coded seating arrangement would be more interesting and effective from many points of view, especially when an event was not sold out. Having a range of colors among empty seats would create the illusion on television of more people in the stadium. Each section of the arena had a range of three to four colors of seating which were installed in a random fashion. It was so well received that when I was commissioned to design the 20,000-seat sports arena adjacent to the Superdome, I used the same system for the arena seating.

In 1975 the Louisiana Superdome received an American Institute of Architects Honor Award. Since it opened on August 3, 1975, it has played host to events ranging from college and professional football, baseball, and basketball games to national conventions and exhibitions to the world's largest circus. In 1981, the Rolling Stones established a record attendance of 87,500 for an indoor event. Six Superbowls have been played there. It holds the Final Four attendance record of 64,959 set in 1987, the same year Pope John Paul II appeared there before 80,000. The National Republican Convention was held there in 1988. It has proven time and again to be a versatile facility which can be transformed overnight for different events.

When we were designing the Superdome, it became obvious that a building of such magnitude would have a considerable impact on the surrounding neighborhood. To ensure that there would be harmony between this massive structure and the valuable commercial land adjacent, we developed a master site plan providing for a Super Block all the way from the arena on Poydras Street to Loyola Avenue. This created a hotel-office building zone connected directly into the Superdome facility. On the hotel site we later designed a hotel for Hyatt of 1,200 rooms (see page 130). We proposed that five office buildings be built on the square, creating a critical mass with an anchor to the Central Business District. In addition, we designed a link connecting the commercial complex to the stadium and allowing a hundred-foot open space between the two, which we believed should be developed as a park. Mayor Landrieu did not agree with the concept for the open space. He felt the real estate was much too valuable and vetoed our recommendation that the open space be preserved. A large shopping mall was built filling in the gap which we had hoped to keep as a green area in the heart of the Central Business District. From a commercial point of view, there is no question that Moon Landrieu was correct; from a city planning point of view, I am still not convinced.

In the first fifteen years alone, the total economic impact of the Superdome to the New Orleans area economy was $3.93 billion. A study prepared for the State of Louisiana concluded that the New Orleans Saints in 2002 had a $402 million impact. The 2002 Super Bowl was estimated to have had a $374 million impact. The economic vision of Governor McKeithen has been realized many times over. Houston's Astrodome, situated farther out of the city, does not have the impact on the surrounding real estate which made the Superdome so financially important to the development of downtown New Orleans. The facility allows the city to compete successfully in areas where it would otherwise never be possible. Without the Superdome, New Orleans could not have hosted the Republican National Convention in 1988, which had a $140 million impact despite the city's depressed economy at the time. Such events also generate national and international publicity with additional economic impact.

The Louisiana Superdome has stood the test of time. Many domes have been built since, but I don't believe any has a better design, and that includes those with retractable roofs. They are trendy and theatrical, but I don't think they make for a better building. The Dome personified New Orleans even before August 29, 2005, but now, thanks to Hurricane Katrina and the Saints' remarkable 2006 season, the Dome is known the world over as a symbol of great tragedy and of almost unbelievable triumph. I never doubted that the Dome could

survive even the strongest hurricane. During construction, the anodized aluminum panel that made up the wall of the Superdome was shipped to St. Louis and subjected to the forces of a wind tunnel to ensure it would survive a direct hit from a strong hurricane. It passed the test. The whole world knows what happened to the roof during the storm, and what happened when angry and frustrated evacuees took out their emotions on the interior of the Dome. But through it all, the building itself stood firm.

The cost to rehabilitate the Dome exceeded what it cost to build it, but it is hard to question the economic and emotional necessity of reopening the stadium. On September 26, 2006, when the Saints rushed onto the field, the crowd shook the Dome with shouts of joy, and there was not a dry eye in the house. Almost four months later, the Saints won another playoff game in the Dome. As a result, the Dome became a symbol once again, of a city rising up from its darkest hour.

A Walk in the Park and along the Lakefront

Dutch Morial, the first African American mayor elected by New Orleans, was one of the most dynamic personalities to serve in this office. He was the first black man to be elected to the state legislature and was a strong supporter of expanding opportunities for minority groups. I admired him very much, and we became close friends; for some time we had a ritual of early-morning walks together on the edge of City Park. It was quite a procession, since usually he would have one or two bodyguards and other political allies as a part of the entourage. We would walk two miles at a relatively fast pace, but it gave us an opportunity to discuss many of the civic problems which he had under consideration at the time.

On one of these walks I suggested something should be done in front of City Hall. Although the City Hall complex,

State Office Building, and Courts Building were constructed around an open park during the 1950s under Chep Morrison's administration, nothing had ever been done to enhance the large expanse of undeveloped green area at the entrance to City Hall. I suggested that it be developed into a park where people from the Central Business District could congregate for brown-bag outdoor lunches and even concerts, giving some life to this unused expanse in the center of Central Business District. Dutch said, "Go ahead and do it!"

With this simple directive, I developed a design which created a promenade from City Hall bisecting the open field, passing the Public Library which we had designed some years before, and even extending the vista down Basin Street to Armstrong Park. Since the land was completely flat, I created contours and two elevated sitting areas topped by a colonnade of oak trees which eventually would be an alley of shade trees over the mounds where people could enjoy concerts performed in an open shelter in the center of the park. As a theme for the shelter, we planned to construct a simple umbrella roof with no sides, the shape of the roof inspired by a beautifully proportioned outbuilding at Melrose Plantation upriver from the city of New Orleans (see page 131). Under the roof we designed an elevated platform with a room below for storage of musical instruments and any other equipment needed to service the activities on the platform. The roof was to be constructed with wood shingles and supported by four columns with ten-foot cantilevers protecting the stage from inclement weather conditions. Landscaping was critical and we used indigenous plants wherever possible, including an alley of live oak trees, clusters of crepe myrtles, and the addition of magnolia trees for shade around the perimeter of the site.

Mayor Morial approved the design in concept and advised us to go forward with getting the necessary building permits, since there were funds available to complete the construction. As it turned out there were not enough funds, but I personally solicited donations from friends in New Orleans and New York as well as made a personal contribution to ensure that the pavilion would be built at the same time as the surrounding landscaping. All seemed to be in order, and I proceeded to present the plans to the proper agencies.

Little did I realize that seven different departments had to approve the design, including the City Planning Commission, the Zoning Commission, the State Planning Agency (since a portion of the land abutted a state office building), the fire marshal (to locate fire hydrants and approve a wood shingle roof in the Central Business District), Parks and Parkways (who would maintain the park after the construction was completed), and Department of Streets (since the approaches crossed two major arteries) A building permit could be issued only after all of the other agencies had been satisfied. Much to my surprise many of these agencies were not particularly in favor of the idea and put up roadblocks at every turn. At long last, after four months of visits, discussions, hearings, and some arm twisting from Mayor Morial, we received our building permit, and at last the park was built. I learned that a simple suggestion on a walk through City Park could develop into a major headache, but the park became an important addition to downtown New Orleans.

Curtis & Davis experienced master planning on a grand scale when we had the opportunity to develop entire complexes and groups of buildings. We designed the campus for the University of New Orleans at the waterfront facing Lake Pontchartrain, on a site donated to Louisiana by the United States Navy. It had been a naval airfield built as a training strip for fledgling pilots during World War II. When we were chosen to design a new basketball arena for the university, we recommended that the building be a multipurpose facility since the volume required for seating and the basketball configuration would be conducive to other types of recreational activities. It was subsequently named Senator Nat Kiefer UNO Lakefront Arena (see page 132).

The Lakefront Arena is a unique structure in many respects. It was designed to be used for intercollegiate basketball, theatrical performances, concerts, lectures, and similar events requiring a seating capacity anywhere from 2,000 to 9,000, depending on the configuration and use. The basketball floor is removable for other types of events, and the portable stage can be expanded or retracted by segments, depending on specific needs. Adjoining the main arena are eight complete locker rooms and special dressing rooms, including two "star suites."

Under one segment of the sloping seating, a large area serves as practice courts for basketball. This space can be divided into separate areas or used as one large practice space. On the south side of the arena under the sloping seating, a major Olympic-sized swimming pool has been provided. Three diving platforms and two movable bridges allow the length of the pool to be adjusted for different swimming events. There are 260 permanent seats adjacent to the swimming pool, but there is ample space provided for an additional 1,500 portable seats for special events. Since the swimming pool has a southern exposure it has been designed with a glass wall and an outdoor area for sunbathing and relaxing between swimming events. The arena also has meeting rooms with adjacent kitchen facilities, ancillary offices for coaches and staff, and exercise rooms.

The footprint of the building covers 5.3 acres; the gross floor area is 146,720 square feet. Over the arena a clear-span carried by major trusses serves as an umbrella protecting the sloping exterior walls from all weather conditions. The building is of steel frame construction within an aluminum and glass envelope. All seats are upholstered, and on the concourse level are emergency medical and first aid rooms, a generous pedestrian area with concessions, toilet facilities, and trophy cases. The upper levels are accessed by two elevators and four major pedestrian ramps.

Because of its excellent capabilities, the arena has been extensively patronized not only by the university but by the community at large.

Saudi Arabia and the End of C&D

In the seventies and eighties, architectural firms in the United States looked to the Middle East, especially to wealthy Saudi Arabia where there was a desire to expand and build. With plenty of money available, the country was a fertile source of exciting architectural commissions. We, along with many others, tried our luck in this country with seemingly unlimited funds for large and unusual projects.

We soon discovered the pitfalls involved in conducting business in a country with vastly different practices and traditions. To work in Saudi Arabia, a firm had to be sponsored by a prince of the Royal Family. In our case, the sponsor, Prince Fahd, was a close personal friend of our Lebanese agent, Elias Farah. Elias was a charming, vivacious, and delightful travel companion, and we became quite good friends. He visited us in New Orleans, showered gifts on my children, and referred to me as his "brother," a term of endearment which was not unusual in this part of the Arab world.

When I arrived in Riyadh, I was assigned a room in the hotel, and Elias informed me that I should stand by until I heard from him. Three days later, he returned from meeting with Prince Fahd with a list of prospective projects from the Ministry of Youth Welfare, whose president general was Prince Faisal. Prince Fahd, the second in command of the ministry, was in charge when Prince Faisal left the country, and this was the time that we were to be available to obtain a commission. We selected a cultural center to be built in Riyadh, with adaptations of the same complex later to be built in Dammam and in Jeddah; thus we would have an opportunity to design three buildings under our one contract. With excitement I returned to New York with the program for these cultural centers in hand. Little did I know what disaster lay ahead.

The three sites were on very different terrains, so we were not able to use the same design in all three locations. We estimated the total costs, including allowances for travel, engineering help, and other incidental expenses and gave the figure to Elias. Our fee was accepted and the ministry prepared an agreement which Elias signed on our behalf. It was completely in Arabic. Elias had it translated for us, but we were uncertain exactly how the contract would be enforced. All began smoothly. We received an initial payment—through Elias—and began developing designs for the cultural centers. Most of this work was done in our New York office, and to meet the Saudis' expectations, we prepared not only preliminary plans, but also a detailed model and a brochure in both Arabic and in English. This was a very expensive procedure for us; however, we were to be reimbursed for this work.

In approximately three months we had our designs, our model, and our brochure ready to present to the president general of Youth Welfare in Riyadh. The design was innovative, a very powerful building with a strong, honest expression of the major elements and respect for the harsh climate with a minimum of exterior openings. All exterior fenestration was shaded, and exterior circulation was protected under canopied walkways.

For the presentation meeting, Nathaniel Curtis joined me on the trip. As luck would have it, Prince Faisal was in the country, and he, not Prince Fahd, received our designs. We arrived at Prince Faisal's office at nine sharp, and his deputy asked us to wait in the outer office until the Prince arrived. At 11:15 we were ushered into his private chambers. The Prince was a very large, imposing man, who gave the impression of undisputed authority. At this particular moment, he did not look pleased. He advised us that he had reviewed our designs, did not approve of them at all, and was very disappointed in what we had done. This was not a very encouraging prospect for us.

Then the Prince complained, "That is the trouble with you British, you just want to do things your own way and do not care about our culture. You have to remember we are not Bedouins—we're civilized people."

At this moment Elias informed the prince, "Your Royal Highness Prince Faisal, these are not English—they are *American* architects."

Prince's countenance changed immediately and the frown became a broad smile. He cordially indicated that we were to be seated and said, "I hope you are enjoying your stay in our country. We want to have friendly relations with the Americans."

Once the ice was broken, he suggested, "Why don't you see if you can come up with a more satisfactory look to the building? If you can bring these drawings to me tomorrow morning, maybe we can resolve whatever differences we have and move forward with these cultural centers."

With this, the Prince's aide ushered us out and took us to the hotel. He advised us that we should have the new drawings by tomorrow morning at nine o'clock. Our task lay before us, and it had to be accomplished between noon on Tuesday and nine o'clock on Wednesday morning. We laid out a work table and spent most of the night hard at work. By the next morning we had six solutions to offer to the Prince. We hoped that one would be satisfactory to his taste. With no sleep and totally exhausted, we returned to the Prince's office only to discover that he had gone on a week long hunting trip. We were advised to wait at the hotel until the Prince returned and granted us another audience.

In five days the Prince returned, but the deputy informed us that it would not be necessary for us to be present; he would take the drawings to the prince. We noted our first, second, and third choices, and the deputy promised to pass on our recommendations. That evening the deputy called to say that the prince had accepted our first choice and that we were free to leave the country and proceed on the basis of the revised design. We left on the first flight out the following day.

With the prince's approval, we completed construction documents and submitted them through Elias to the ministry's construction division. We were then informed that the funds for the building had not yet been appropriated and that the ministry would hold the plans until that time. We were partially paid for the work which we had completed. What we did not know at the time was that there was room after room after room of completed plans, models, and brochures awaiting construction funding for a large portion of work that was never to be realized, that a large portion of the buildings designed by foreign architects were never to be completed projects, and that a large portion of the design fees were never to be paid.

Subsequently our agent approached us with another commission, a health spa on an oasis called Huf Huf in the desert northeast of Riyadh. The program was very elaborate, with health facilities for men and women all completely isolated from each other. The spas were to include an entire community with facilities for housing, feeding, and entertaining the guests. Curtis was to be the partner-in-charge of the health

spa, and the work would be done in New Orleans and New York. The drawings were quite extensive, and we proceeded with construction documents, creating obligations to engineers and consultants without obtaining interim payments as we did with the cultural centers. When we presented our bill (approximately $7 million dollars), we were told that the payments would be forthcoming, but we would be required to justify all of our expenses.

By this time we realized that getting money from the Saudis was not going to be easy and that not being paid a bill of this magnitude could bankrupt our firm. I stayed in the States to fend off creditors, while Curtis went to Saudi Arabia to collect the funds. His intended stay of only a few days dragged into eight weeks of frustrated effort. To our dismay we learned that within that country there is no opportunity to sue or make demands for payment of any sort. Any request for reimbursement must go directly through agents of the royal family. We enlisted the assistance of the United States ambassador to Saudi Arabia (former governor of South Carolina), John C. West, who promised to intercede with the king. To Curtis's credit, he did manage to obtain slightly more than $3 million (less than half of what we were owed) to pay the banks, our engineers, and other creditors, large and small. The effect of this catastrophe upon our practice was beyond repair, and we were either going to have to close down the office or develop an association with another firm to carry on.

It so happened that a large California architectural and engineering firm, Daniel, Mann, Johnson, & Mendenhall, who were strongly oriented in engineering but wished to expand their architectural capabilities, offered to assist us in our financial dilemma. I was eager to reach an accord with them and negotiated a merger which in all truth was the acquisition of our firm by the California group. They were financially strong, with projects worldwide as well as throughout the United States. This takeover saved us and especially myself from financial disaster. DMJM, as they were called, were most gracious and fair in offering both Curtis and me positions as vice presidents in the firm with handsome salaries and interesting responsibilities. I was particularly eager to reach this agreement, since I had pledged all of our personal securities, both from myself and my wife, to fend off the banks from declaring us insolvent. This merger, along with the money we received from Saudi Arabia, would cover our personal pledges. Curtis did not have that kind of personal exposure since all of the stocks and bonds pledged as collateral belonged to my wife and me.

As it finally developed, as soon as the papers were executed, I became a senior vice president of Daniel, Mann, Johnson & Mendenhall. Curtis resigned from the firm, since by his own admission he was not interested in becoming associated with a large conglomerate—more to the point, he did not feel that DMJM was treating us fairly. I had a completely different perspective of the matter.

This was the sad demise of Curtis & Davis, which over the years had grown from a three-man operation to a major architectural and engineering firm, and a partnership that had lasted from 1947 to 1978. At the peak of our expansion, we were a four-office operation with headquarters in New Orleans, a relatively permanent office in New York, and offices in London and Berlin.

In my new position I was responsible for the operation of the New Orleans office, which was known as DMJM Curtis & Davis, and I also assisted in developing architectural capabilities in many of the other offices around the country and abroad. I also had a cubicle in the headquarters office on Wilshire Boulevard in Los Angeles. As a member of the board I oversaw the selection of architects for projects and approved all of the designs. It was a very pleasant but not terribly challenging experience for me. For ten years with DMJM I quite candidly was paid handsomely for a minimum amount of productive work, and as soon as I reached the ten-year period which permitted me to be tenured, I resigned from the firm and received the funds which I had earned through their very generous retirement plan.

When I became a part of the DMJM firm, one of the conditions of settlement was that I would receive a block of DMJM stock, which I held until DMJM was acquired by Ashland Oil. They bought 100 percent of the DMJM stock at what I considered to be an exorbitant figure, and it was very much a windfall for me personally. A few years after I had left the firm, Ashland determined that this was not such a good acquisition for them and they sold the company back to the DMJM employees.

On My Own

I'm very enthusiastic about my present practice. My shop, Arthur Q. Davis FAIA and Partners, includes some of the architects from the Curtis & Davis office, including one associate with whom I have worked for over sixteen years. My secretary, Kathy Driscoll Lopez, has been with me for thirty-four years, and another associate has returned after having retired from practice for twelve years. With these tried and true veterans as a nucleus, we've built a very strong staff and energetically expanded our practice.

Among our projects has been the development of long-term master planning for an entire new community of approximately 20,000 people being built in the rainforest jungle of Indonesia on the island of New Guinea in Inirianjaya, its largest province. This was a challenging project. Kuala Kencana is not a company town, although the impetus was furnished by Freeport-McMoRan to accommodate the needs of employees working on copper and gold mines in the vicinity (see page 133). Perhaps the most important and challenging aspect of the planning was to keep the specific needs of the Indonesians as an integral part of our design process. As has been the case with many of the important commissions I have received, that of Kuala Kencana grew out of a very minor request. Freeport-McMoRan engaged us to consult on some modifications to a small ninety-room inn to be built adjacent to the new town site and which was to be operated by the Sheraton chain. We suggested ways the building could better relate to the rainforest and the surrounding environment. Freeport accepted our recommendations, and the inn was modified accordingly. The original designs for the inn, as well as the early master plan for the new town, were developed by Helmuth, Obatta, and Kassabalm of St. Louis. As the town developed and the need for additional coordination and creative insight became more demanding, we were requested to take over the lead in design control and work with the Indonesian officials who would eventually be required to approve all aspects of the town.

Early urban designs for the new town were based upon conventional grid street patterns. We believed that the town should be more integrated with the environment. At Freeport's suggestion we prepared an alternate design which was much more organic, with neighborhoods surrounded by local vegetation and connected to other neighborhoods by paths through the rainforest. We also recommended a ring road with all of the other facilities serviced by this road, allowing future expansion. Our scheme was approved by the Freeport management group and adopted as the final design for the new town.

The housing included units for officials as well as workers involved in the mining operation. The attractive and efficient workers' houses were designed to withstand the elements including the torrential rains, termites, and other deteriorations of the exterior surface, both walls and roofs. Even though these homes were relatively modest in size, we were advised that in all cases it was necessary to include a room for a live-in servant, as there was ample labor available and this was common practice. We initially designed bedrooms with typical closets, but we eliminated the closets when we learned that Indonesians preferred chests and armoires. The bathrooms were conventional with the exception of the toilets. Typical Eastern toilets used a recessed design, so we were advised to provide an equal number of Western and Eastern toilets. As it turned out, the people eventually preferred the Western style, and we had to replace many units to accommodate this change in attitude.

Government buildings and office buildings of other companies were also a part of the new town as were a shopping center, a Christian church and a mosque, and a golf club with an eighteen-hole golf course built into the rainforest, a very dramatic and exciting course designed by Ben Crenshaw and Bill Koore with fairways cut through majestic trees. While the course was under construction, one had to be alert to possible intruders such as fifteen-foot pythons and other indigenous creatures. Kuala Kencana is halfway up a mountain in the center of Inirianjaya where the largest gold mine in the world and a major copper mine are located. The mountain is in rugged terrain close to the equator, but because of the altitude, the peaks are covered by snow during twelve months of the year. The original natives in this part of Inirianjaya live the same lifestyle that they have had for hundreds of years. A native man wears no clothes with the exception of a gourd over his penis, and women wear no clothes with the exception of a small brush over their groins. They live in thatched houses with no windows and one door but still build fires inside the dwellings. We were asked by the government to consider designing some new houses for the natives but they resisted. Their way of life has not yet been affected by the workers coming in from other parts of Indonesia or the United States and they preferred living as they always have.

Our opportunity to design the New Orleans Arena came through Governor Edwin Edwards, a dynamic, charismatic politician who was able to speak on almost any subject without any notes and with minimum preparation beforehand. I arranged for him to speak before the Louisiana Chapter of the American Institute of Architects and he talked about architecture in a way that made us all proud to be a part of the profession. After Curtis & Davis merged with Daniel, Mann, Johnson & Mendenhall, he also agreed to give a lecture to our combined offices of approximately 250 people at a meeting in Las Vegas. It was no secret that the governor enjoyed gambling, and he was happy to travel there to speak. Once again he acquitted himself magnificently as he spoke effortlessly about Las Vegas, California, Louisiana, and other parts of the world where DMJM/C&D was then doing major projects, including Saudi Arabia, Japan, and Indonesia to name just a few.

The State of Louisiana decided to build a sports facility for ice hockey and professional basketball. Although the Superdome can seat 80,000 to 100,000, depending on the event, its size is overpowering for certain concerts, circuses, and events that would require anywhere from a 15,000 to 20,000–seat facility. I very much wanted to design the New Orleans Arena since my firm had planned the Superdome and the UNO facility. The final decision was up to Governor Edwards. Although the Louisiana Stadium and Exposition District (LSED) was responsible for selecting the architect, firms interested in a large state project were requested to submit qualifications to an Architecture Selection Committee (usually five people) made up of architects, clients, and members of the

State Building Authority. The governor controlled at least three votes of the committee, so in almost all instances, the firm that he favored would be awarded the contract. Everyone knew this, and this was just the way it was in Louisiana for the conduct of much of the state business. With this in mind I requested an appointment with the governor at the mansion in Baton Rouge. I had carefully prepared my remarks as to why I thought my firm would be the logical choice, but he interrupted me after two sentences. He told me that the decision was already being made, and it would be a waste of my time and his for him to hear any dissertation on the subject of my qualifications. He then invited me for lunch, and we had no further mention of the architectural commission for the sports arena.

The next day I received a call from the committee informing me that we had been chosen to design the New Orleans Arena. It was as simple as that. That was the way Governor Edwards operated. He controlled almost all state construction, and in most cases he selected qualified people. There was never any mention of kickback or payment to him or any of his cronies—we were awarded the contract merely because the governor thought we were qualified. He had a reputation of expecting something in return, but nothing like this materialized on this project. I am pleased to say that we designed a very handsome facility with no interference at all from the governor's office.

Unfortunately that was not always the case; a number of deals of a much larger and comprehensive nature embroiled the governor in some rather shady transactions. At this moment he is paying the price by serving ten years at a federal prison in Texas. In many ways he was a very capable governor who did a lot of good, but sadly his questionable deeds tarnished his reputation beyond repair.

When we began the New Orleans Arena, we had a budget

of approximately $85 million and at that time the facility was intended for ice hockey and basketball. Much commentary and controversy arose over the expense, given the fact that the city at that time had no professional basketball team and ice hockey was an unlikely sport in a subtropical city. After the facility was completed, New Orleans was able to attract the Hornets, an NBA team formerly based in Charlotte. Despite the fact that the arena was equipped for ice hockey, the demanding schedule of professional basketball left little time for other sports, and the LSED Board decided to terminate the agreement with the ice hockey team. When the Hornets arrived in New Orleans, additional locker rooms and concession stands were needed. The final cost for the entire project was $114 million.

The excellent acoustics in the arena make it a viable facility for all kinds of events in addition to professional basketball. When the Arena Football League awarded a franchise to the city, the natural place to house the New Orleans Voo-Doo was the arena, and their first year they were conference champions. Unusual features include the colored seating similar to that developed for the Superdome and an innovative structural system, one used in bridges but never before in buildings. Two major concrete ribs approximately twelve feet deep were poured on the ground and then collected by cranes spanning the width of the building. These ribs carried the major load and therefore the other roof members, all made of the steel and of a lesser dimension, could be more efficiently erected. The building façade is sheathed in enamel panels in shades of green, and the roof is aluminum. Both surfaces are permanent and indestructible. One of the problems we encountered at the Superdome was that the roof was subject to different forms of vandalism, including bullets fired from the expressway and the housing project beyond. Although the bullets do not penetrate the surface, they are a

great inconvenience. With the aluminum surface of the New Orleans Sports Arena, this condition does not exist.

The arena is a beautiful, efficient, no-frills structure (see page 134). One of our concerns was to design a building that would harmonize with the adjacent Superdome but not be considered a smaller copy of the larger facility. Instead of having a building that was basically round, the design exterior is a series of vertical planes with a different color and a different texture, but in our opinion create a harmonious juxtaposition of the two forms. The Superdome is completely enclosed while the arena has large areas of glass facing toward downtown and toward the Central Business District. The two facilities share parking for many major events, and with pedestrian connections at two levels, they interrelate functionally and aesthetically. Because of the efficiency of the structural design and other considerations such as shared air conditioning (the arena needs 2500 tons as opposed to 9000 tons for the Superdome), it was one of the least expensive buildings among all of stadiums in the NBA and is still considered a first-rate facility at a bargain basement price.

The sports facilities I have had a hand in designing have given New Orleans some of the most comprehensive venues of any city in the United States, whether it be for sports or entertainment. The Superdome seats 80,000–100,000 people, the New Orleans Arena seats 18,000–20,000, and the UNO facility seats 9,000, so there is an appropriate venue no matter what the event.

About twelve years ago I decided to reestablish ties to the Tulane School of Architecture, and I agreed to teach a seminar course to fourth- and fifth-year students. Officially called Divergent Forces Affecting the Design of Contemporary Buildings, the course was an opportunity to expose the students to the outside forces in play when designing a modern building in today's society. After four or five years, I became too involved in other work and travel to continue, but in 2004, I went back and once again taught a seminar course to the upper class of students. I also agreed to sponsor the Arthur Q. and Mary Davis Visiting Critic which, as it turned out, was a rather expensive program since most of the people I wanted to invite were from other parts of the United States or overseas. We invited such celebrated architects as Harry Seidler from Sydney, Australia, who was a classmate of mine at Harvard in 1946. I was also able to entice Charles Correa from India, who spent two very enjoyable weeks at Tulane and made a strong impression on the students.

Among others I invited was Liu Xiao-Shi, the chief city planner from Beijing, who reciprocated by inviting me to give a course at Tsinghua University which is China's equivalent to MIT. For two weeks I gave lectures every day to Tsinghua students on different subjects, mostly relating to American architecture, with slides and photographs. The courses were presented in English with Chinese translations so that an hour lecture usually ended up being a little over two and a half hours long, but everyone seemed to be very enchanted with what I had to offer.

While I was in Beijing, the students were preparing to enter a national competition on a design of a contemporary bridge and ancillary facilities. The competition was open to all students from all the universities in China. I worked with our people giving them a constructive critique. I am pleased to report that Tsinghua University students won first prize in the national competition. I was graciously given some credit for this honor, but mainly it was the students who performed so well.

When I was giving my lectures, I talked about the structural systems of some of the buildings we had designed, including the IBM building in Pittsburgh, where the exterior wall was the truss that supported the building; there were no interior columns. At the end of the class one of the students came up to my desk and showed me a picture of the Pittsburgh IBM building in the Chinese textbook on contemporary buildings around the world. I was gratified to discover that one of our buildings described in my course to the Chinese students was actually included in a text book on the other side of the world.

My course was so successful that Dr. Li, the chairman of the University, asked me to return to give a second set of lectures, not in Beijing, but near the Tibetan border. I indicated to him that I would be pleased to return, but on the conditions that I be permitted to visit the great Tibetan capital of Lhasa and tour some of the monasteries and other imposing buildings of that remote but fascinating country. When I returned, I lectured in Cheng Du and I was given a guide, a young student who had served in one of the monasteries in Tibet as a student monk. With his guidance I was able to travel to Tibet and see all of the important buildings. The great Potala in Lhasa was even more exciting than anything I had expected from the photographs. It was a massive structure but beautifully detailed. One unusual feature that I never expected to find was that the colors used on the Potala as well as on some of the other temples and monasteries were warmer colors, reminiscent of Native American color schemes prevalent in the western part of the United States. I was pleased to have the opportunity to visit Tibet before the influx of Chinese, who have now dominated the environment with ugly makeshift dormitories for workers imported into Lhasa. These newer structures are not in harmony with the traditional buildings of Tibet. Most of monasteries we visited have since been destroyed by the Chinese, but the monks, by sheer will and desire to restore some of the traditional architecture of this fascinating country, are now rebuilding a few with government support.

A President's Visit

Probably the most important meeting I have had with a president was with Bill Clinton, who came to my house in the Warehouse District of New Orleans to raise funds for Congressman Bill Jefferson, who was running for reelection at the time. It is quite interesting when a president of the United States pays a visit to a home. The security requirements began two days before, and although he spent only a few hours with me, the security precautions included snipers on the roof, the removal of all private vehicles from our building, the use of trained German shepherd dogs policing the grounds before and after the president's visit, and of course the FBI surveillance during his stay. He personally was a dynamic, vivacious, and outgoing person and superb politician. Approximately fifty people attended our little soirée, and he personally visited with each of us. Since he had spent a good deal of time in New Orleans, he has many friends and colleagues there, many of whom attended the party at my home. I have a large collection of architectural books as well as historically important first editions, and the president took time to review my collection. He made special note of the fact that we each had a copy of a signed first edition of Mark Twain.

His speech to the group was delightful and made a strong point for his reason to visit. He did it beautifully, which gave everyone the impression that they were expected to make a generous contribution. He raised a considerable amount of money in a very short visit, well in excess of $150,000. Since I was the host, I was required to introduce him to the group, but I was instructed to not get involved in any political comments and to keep the introduction as low key as possible. I took this to heart, but once I had the podium I informed the audience that I had been instructed to not ask the President any questions which might be embarrassing; however, since this was a rare opportunity, I did decide to ask him something very personal. At this point I could see that my wife and the other members of my family looked very concerned that I might do something terrible and disgrace us all. The question I asked the president, since he was a rabid golfer, was if he used the same handicap when he played with friends as when he played with visiting dignitaries when it might be important for him to make a good impression. Everyone was relieved because this was not a particularly political comment.

I am on the board of the National World War II Museum founded by Stephen A. Ambrose and was involved in the selection of its architects and approval of their designs. One of the attractions at the museum is a section where the public can enter booths and listen to veterans relate their own World War II experiences. I am happy to say mine are included. Presently I am involved in its expansion, a project of more than $300 million.

On July 12, 2002, I received the Medal of Honor from the American Institute of Architects, Louisiana Chapter. My firm continues to stay active. We have completed and implemented a master plan for the visual enhancement of the entire Port of New Orleans, including signage, renovation of warehouses, color coordination, and landscaping. A linear port, ten miles in length bordering on the Mississippi River, the Port of New Orleans has the potential to become one of the most efficient and beautiful ports in the United States. We have also completed the construction of a branch bank and are now planning a second branch bank for the largest banking group in Louisiana.

The fifteen years that my family spent living in the authentic Creole cottage, a truly important historic building, were very gratifying. My wife and I now reside in the Warehouse District adjacent to the Mississippi River in a furniture warehouse, one of the first restorations of a warehouse in New Orleans to condominium living. The first level of the four-story building has been converted to parking for the living units above. The second and third floors were restored as four or five units per floor. The top floor accommodates a large rooftop penthouse. Some of the units are very traditional, some contemporary, and some quite raw. All were finished with great detail and loving care (see page 135).

I intended my unit to express the tradition of the warehouse but at the same time include the amenities for con-

temporary luxurious living. The warehouse was built with brick firewalls every twenty-one feet, so it was necessary to cut doors in major partitions between the different areas. Originally the floors were old, dilapidated pine, the interior walls were brick, and the ceiling was exposed wood timbers. I elected to expose the brick walls, I saved some of the timbers over skylights where I placed indoor gardens, and on top of the old wood floors I installed beautiful Vermont slate. In some of the other areas I added traditional knotty-pine floors of beautiful textures and natural colors. While this condo was being built, I was restoring a restaurant in the French Quarter on the Mississippi River, and we employed an artist to paint one of the ceilings in the restaurant with a blue sky and clouds. I employed the same artist to paint the ceilings of my living room and dining room in the same fashion. The unit is approximately four thousand square feet and extends from South Peters Street to Fulton Street, giving the illusion of spaciousness with both living and dining at one end of the space to master bedroom at the far end going from city block to city block. The unit actually has three exposures and two balconies.

The condominium has a master bedroom, a study, a guest bedroom, a vestibule, music room, dining room, a spacious living room with fireplace, a Pullman kitchen, and a maid's

quarters located in the rear of the kitchen and laundry areas. It is a very comfortable and pleasant place to live, and I am looking forward to spending many years here.

At approximately the same time the warehouse was being restored, we had a commission to build a country home for Dr. Bhansali, a physician originally from Bombay, India. The beautiful setting for the home was near Poplarville, Mississippi, on a mound overlooking a meadow with a manmade pond. Dr. Bhansali and his wife, an Indian princess, were art collectors, and we designed the house specifically to showcase their extensive collection of bronze sculptures and other artifacts from seventeenth- and eighteenth-century India. The house itself utilizes large open spaces—the living room is eighteen feet tall, and the dining room is twelve feet tall. The warm textures of natural woods and large expanses of glass further contribute to the spacious quality. Dr. Bhansali uses the house on weekends to train his thoroughbred racehorses. The building, the artwork, and the people who live there have been extensively featured in numerous publications.

In Conclusion

After over sixty years of designing schools, hospitals, churches, office buildings, libraries, prisons, banks, public buildings, and innumerable private residences, perhaps it would be appropriate to evaluate the wide-ranging scope of our practice. We have designed works of importance both architecturally and historically, frequently producing buildings that served the community as a whole as well as our client. This would include the Jewish Community Center, still functioning quite satisfactorily after many years of hard use. The JCC is not only handsome but works very well and is a tribute to the design since the clients are able to live, work, and enjoy the environment. Other projects that functioned very well include 1) the Louisiana Superdome, one of the best multipurpose stadiums in the world, compared in size to the Coliseum in Rome; 2) the Berlin Medical Center, one of the most advanced teaching hospitals in Europe; 3) Louisiana State Penitentiary in Angola, a correctional institution conceived in the Federal Bureau of Prisons classification system; 4) the Louisiana Power and Light building, enclosed in an aluminum skin that protects from the elements; 5) the

New Orleans Arena, a truly stunning building with an intriguing ribbed structural system; 6) the Automotive Life insurance building on Canal Street in New Orleans, truly a gem; 7) Thomy Lafon Elementary School, a unique but endangered environment; and 8) St. Francis Cabrini Church, one of the finest examples of contemporary ecumenical architecture in America.

Sadly, many of our best works have been mutilated or destroyed. We have had to suffer the loss of the Rivergate Convention Center, with its graceful thin-shell long-span structure. The demolition of the Rivergate diminished not only the downtown New Orleans area, but the city as a whole. Another disappointment for us was the loss of the United States Embassy in Saigon, which served as a haven during the severe fighting in the Vietnam War. The embassy was well designed to protect the personnel in the building under the most trying circumstances. The demolition of the St. Francis Xavier Cabrini Church in New Orleans was a disaster for architecture and a personal one for me as well. It was one of our most beautiful buildings. It should never have been destroyed.

A number of our original building designs were never completed as conceived, but compromised to meet conditions beyond our control. The gold anodized aluminum screen we envisioned for the New Orleans Public Library never materialized, and the fenestration of the Forrestal Federal Office Building in Washington, D.C. was substantially altered from our initial concept. *The Family Group*, the exceptional piece of contemporary sculpture mounted on the New Orleans Parish Courthouse, has completely disappeared. Over time, some of our buildings, notably the George Washington Carver High School and Thomy Lafon Elementary School, were detrimentally modified by other hands.

However, on the positive side we were able to develop new and innovative structural systems such as the lift-slab process at the Louisiana State Penitentiary; the freestanding, column-free spans of the IBM building in Pittsburgh; the concrete arches on the New Orleans Arena, an architectural element used only on bridges before this construction; the thin shell roof of the Rivergate; and the six-hundred-foot clear-span of the Superdome.

We also experimented extensively in the use of other creative architectural features in colors, textures, forms, and spacial concepts, among them the aluminum skin on the Superdome, the porcelain enamel panels on the New Orleans Arena, sun screens in both masonry and metal, strong colors on the Island of Aruba in the Caribbean, and distinctive brick patterns on PS 201 in Harlem, New York, on Cabrini Church, and on many residences.

Our practice was worldwide in scope, including designs for a new town in Indonesia; a hotel in St. Andrews, Scotland, for British Railways; the Ambulatory Care and Research Center in Bethesda, Maryland; a medical hospital and teaching center in West Berlin, Germany; a cultural center in Saudi Arabia; and banks in Athens and Berlin. We were fortunate to have had the opportunities to create exciting buildings in exotic locations around the world.

As architects, we have a significant obligation to our society, to our profession, to the arts, and to our fellow men. It is our God-given directive to use our talent to improve our environment through the creation of better buildings, neighborhoods, cities, and regions, and we must accept responsibility for the goals we set for our designs. The buildings we have designed throughout our many years of practice reflect our intent to build a more harmonious world through better architecture.

How fortunate I am to have been a part of such a noble profession.

Projects

Giraffe house at Audubon Park Zoo, New Orleans, 1960.

With brick projections extending from the surface, when the sun shown on it at different times of the day, the façade appeared to imitate the patterned skin of a giraffe. Photograph by Frank Lotz Miller.

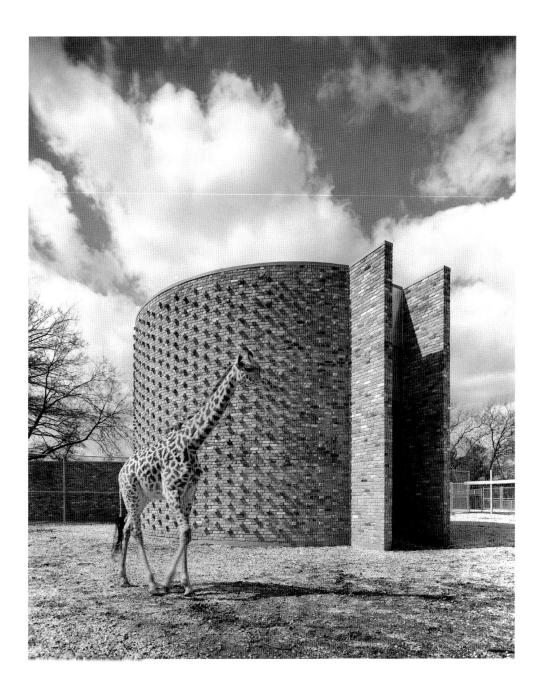

Residence of Edgar B. Stern, Jr., Old Metairie, 1956.

The swimming pool at the Stern house began at the terrace off the living room area with a small body of water with curving sculptural steps following its contours. This small pool expanded into a larger body of water, a "lake," which accommodated a toadstool pedestal for drinks and hors d'oeuvres. From this large expanse, the pool curved around a beautiful old cypress tree into a smaller area that we referred to as the "meditation pond." The lake is approximately fifty by eighty feet and has a very sensuous shape.

**Residence of Dr. Morris Shushan,
New Orleans, 1949.**

Photographs by Frank Lotz Miller.

Residence of Walter B. Moses, Jr., New Orleans.

The design for the Moses house was quite compact in plan: All of the major rooms including living room, dining room, kitchen, and three bedrooms were on the second level, and the ground floor was devoted to services, mechanical equipment, a recreation room, and a two-car garage. The entire structure is reinforced concrete with a stucco finish. On the street façade under the windows in a recessed frame we introduced blue and white Mexican tile, adding a texture and color to what otherwise was the rigid geometry of the building.

Residence of Julian and Ina Steinberg, New Orleans, 1960.

The Steinberg home has a flat roof, more than fifteen feet above grade. The difference in levels is achieved by changing the height of the floors, elevating or depressing, depending upon the overall spatial effect desired. The house opened into its private garden patios. Since the site was on a corner, we felt that privacy was essential, and at the same time, that tradition of the French and Spanish residences—which almost always had enclosed patios turning their backs to the street—needed to be respected.

The most important design decision we made was that from all angles within the house, the Steinbergs would be able to enjoy a view of the massive oak trees without sacrificing their privacy.

To achieve this objective, we permitted the roof to float above the windowless walls, which incidentally were constructed of French Quarter soft-rose-colored, used brick laid up in decorative patterns, a concept we utilized very effectively in future church designs. The soft-burned, warm-colored brick gave us a palette with almost limitless opportunity. The Steinberg house truly proved that materials from the past could be used effectively in a contemporary way. Photograph by Frank Lotz Miller.

Patio and interior views of Steinberg residence. Photographs by Frank Lotz Miller.

William J. Guste Homes, New Orleans.

The high rise provided an efficient and acceptable housing for single occupants and the elderly. The larger family dwellings in the low rise, opening onto the play fields, also worked well. In fact, the project was so well received that the next public housing project, Fisher Housing Project—to be built on the west bank of the Mississippi River—was a mirror image of our design which, although other architects were commissioned to do the work, copied our concept. Photograph by Frank Lotz Miller.

Saint Frances Xavier Cabrini School, New Orleans.

Cabrini School was designed from a finger plan, with a series of classroom wings connected by a corridor. On the opposite side of the corridor from the classrooms were the administration, cafeteria, gymnasium, and other ancillary facilities. Each finger had four to six classrooms with courtyards. The one-story design allowed ample light and air with landscaping and play areas between the classrooms. On the south side we opened the classroom with an all-glass wall, which was revolutionary at that time, facing onto the play areas. On the north side high windows and a clear story faced north to capture the north light and permit complete cross ventilation to keep the classrooms cool. This was long before there was any thought of air conditioning public schools. The south wall of glass was protected from direct sunlight by an eight-foot overhang, so there was good, balanced light entering the classroom both from the north and the south. Photograph by Frank Lotz Miller.

Thomy Lafon Elementary School, New Orleans, 1954.

For the single-level Lafon Elementary School, we developed a long, thin classroom wing, gracefully bent to avoid monotony. Each classroom had two walls of specially tinted, heat-resistant glass, both north and south. The entire classroom block was raised fourteen feet off the ground, giving the covered play area the full length of the school. For the kindergarten, we designed a sculptural ramp so that the children could access the kindergarten areas without having to climb any steps. In the center of the ramp, local artist Jack Hastings designed a piece of play sculpture that the children could climb on and enjoy visually from the kindergarten level as well as from the ground. This was a school without corridors, and every pair of classrooms had access to an exit stair, thus eliminating nonproductive areas such as the conventional corridors anywhere in the entire school. Between each set of classrooms we located the stairway and toilet facilities so that the entire ground level was opened as a covered play area. The only areas that were on grade were the cafeteria, which doubled as a small auditorium, and its kitchen—as well as the necessary administrative space for the principal and teachers. Photograph by Frank Lotz Miller.

Since the Lafon school came in well under budget, we were able to convince the school board to fund a ceramic tile mural in the downstairs entrance hall to the school as well as the outdoor sculpture at the foot of the kindergarten ramp. Photographs by Leon Trice.

The George Washington Carver Elementary, Junior, and Senior High School, New Orleans, 1957.

This consolidated school incorporated the concept of shared community facilities such as cafeterias, gymnasiums, and administration offices. Photographs by Frank Lotz Miller.

Intermediate School 201, New York City, 1967.

PS 201 was the first air-conditioned school in New York, and the exterior, windowless classrooms opened onto a central court. The illusion of being indoors was relieved by the inner courtyard.

Science Building, Tulane University, 1960.

Sako Clinic, Raceland, Louisiana, 1967.

The clinic, located in a flood zone of the Mississippi, was elevated four feet off the ground. Surviving severe rainstorms and hurricanes, it was never damaged, and water never reached the main level of the clinic. In order to protect the glass areas of the clinic from the sun and rain, we devised an exterior shading element constructed of terra cotta flue tile, which was manufactured for chimneys, laid up in a vertical pattern. The exterior of the building was composed of a series of solid windowless panels. The flue tile cast shadows and patterns on the glass wall of the waiting room and Dr. Sako's private office. The building was beautiful in its simplicity and was our first use of clay tile. Dr. Sako is a Japanese American pediatrician. The office design has a distinct Oriental appearance.

Caribe Building, Canal Street, New Orleans, 1958.

We were so convinced that a clay tile screen was a sound approach to sun control that we used this concept for all four elevations of our own office building. Especially in the evening, with the lights shining through the masonry elements, the screen takes on a lacy appearance. Photographs by Frank Lotz Miller.

James V. Forrestal Building, Washington, D.C., 1970.

The plan for this Department of Defense building was to include approximately two million square feet of office space plus food facilities for 2,500 people and a concealed underground parking structure for 1,200 cars. We were presented with a site that was divided almost down the middle by 10th Street—a wide boulevard leading to a series of government buildings terminating in a cul-de-sac—with the major access of the building facing Independence Avenue. The challenge was to design a homogeneous building that would span 10th Street but still provide major access through and under our structure. We decided that since our building was to span the street, the major office component should float thirty-five feet above the street and across the entire site, permitting us to open the ground level with an important entrance to the building. The remainder of the office requirements were to be housed in a solid block with a central courtyard placed on one side of 10th Street and connected to the floating office block on Independence by a series of bridges at each level.

James V. Forrestal Building
under construction.

Towbin Healthcare Center, Veterans Administration Hospital, North Little Rock, Arkansas.

Ambulatory Care and Research Center of the National Institute of Health, Bethesda, Maryland.

Our design needed to interface with the existing hospital, a typical H-shaped twelve-story structure in red brick, the building material of all of the older buildings on the NIH campus. We proposed a new block completely divorced from the existing hospital with the exception of bridge connections at each level. This approach was accepted, but then the question of façade arose. After reviewing seven different façade designs, we persuaded the NIH that a glass cube reflecting the forms of the existing hospital and the surrounding environment would be the proper solution. Credits: © 1983 Arnold Kramer, Washington, D.C.

Front entry of Ambulatory Care and Reseach Center.

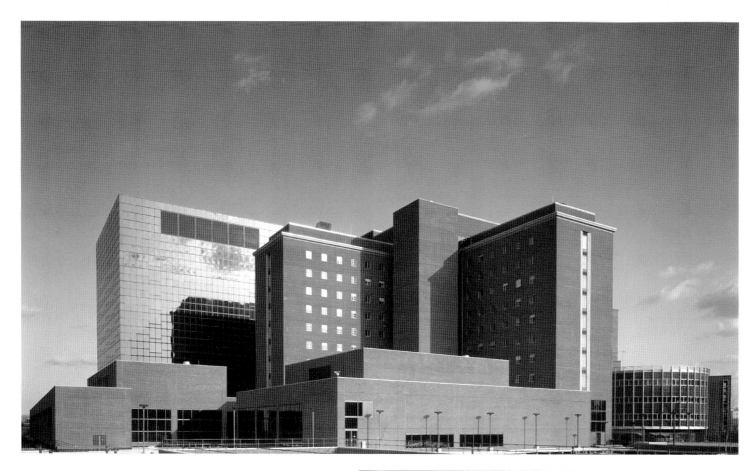

Rear view (with later additions) of
Ambulatory Care and Research Center
of the National Institute of Health.

Lecture hall.

United States Embassy, Saigon.

Our original design included a sun screen element in cast cement which comprised a series of rectangles laid in staggered patterns. The basic unit was approximately fourteen inches square and was designed in the form of a Vietnamese stylized antique coin. Attached to the rectangle was a series of projections in an abstract pattern that created an overall fabric to the sun screen. Such decorative amenities, however, were abandoned when hostilities intervened and the U.S. Navy Seabees were called on to finish construction. A simple rectilinear tile with no design or pattern was cast on the site and installed onto the building. The Seabees did an excellent job, and the embassy was very sound with all elements of security within the building carried out meticulously and in accordance with our designs. Photograph by Frank Lotz Miller.

Original design before modification by the U.S. Navy Seabees.

Personnel were forced to evacuate by helicopter from the embassy compound when Saigon fell. Photographs by Frank Lotz Miller.

Louisiana State Penitentiary, Angola, 1956.

The dining halls, kitchen, and administrative centers for the entire complex were located in the center of the facility. Because of the juxtaposition of the housing units for maximum-, medium-, and minimum-security inmates, we were able to feed the entire institution in one central location out of one kitchen and in two major dining facilities housed under a very graceful double arch.

From the air, the penitentiary at Angola beautifully expresses the functions of the different elements of the design while at the same time creating a beautiful abstract pattern. This view was published on the cover of a Japanese architectural magazine. Photographs by Frank Lotz Miller.

Dining hall, Angola.

The walkway reflects the use of the lift-slab construction technique employed in building the Angola facility.

Cell block, Angola.

Maximum-security inmates were placed in conventional cells, but the exterior walls of the cellblocks were louvered glass windows so that all of the cells would be ventilated and have visual access to the exterior. Since the maximum-security cellblocks were stacked on three levels with a central core, the inmates were not able to reach the exterior louvered windows. Thus security was adequate, but at the same time, the dark interior of typical maximum-security cellblocks was eliminated. The design was as simple and basic as possible: a central core for plumbing, utilities, and ventilation; the cellblock; the inmates' walkways on three levels; and the exterior wall three stories high but not connected to the walkways. The area was enclosed within double fencing with a barbed-wire cap and its own set of guard towers at strategic points around the periphery.

The medium-security compound was designed in H-shaped buildings with a control point at the center. These four wings were also simple rectilinear one-story blocks which could be divided into separate rooms for single, double, or triple occupancy since the petitions were nonstructural. The medium-security housing was also protected by double chainlink fencing with barbed-wire caps and guard towers.

The minimum-security housing was almost identical to the medium security, except that most of the inmates were in open dormitories with a central station at the center of the H. A single chainlink fence with the appropriate guard towers afforded the necessary enclosure for the inmates.

There were no prison walls and therefore the entire complex gave the impression of a series of buildings set into a great expansive openness, which indeed was the case. At one time the site, a great open pasture, had been an exceedingly large sugar cane plantation located on the bend of the Mississippi River. The 18,000 acres of farmland in West Feliciana Parish was at the instep of the boot of the state of Louisiana and flanked by the Tunica Hills, the beginnings of a rise in elevation from the flat delta land extending down through the southern portion of the state. It was an ideal setting for a correctional institution since it was bounded on two sides by the Mississippi River and the other two sides by the densely wooded hills. An inmate who might escape from the prison complex would either be required to swim the Mississippi River, which would be no mean feat, or work his way through the impenetrable terrain of the Tunica Hills. Very few escapees have been able to survive these very difficult natural deterrents, and the rate of recovery for capturing escaped inmates is almost 100 percent.

Perhaps the most innovative contribution to the construction of Angola was the use of a lift slab, a new building technique we discovered in Texas. The entire institution, with the exception of the dining hall, was built by an adaptation of this structural system. It required that a slab be poured directly on the ground with only perimeter form work; a second slab would be poured directly on top of the first with a wax membrane between the two; if a third slab were needed, this would be poured over the second with the wax membrane once again separating the second from the third slab. The only form work would be the exterior form around the perimeter. Before the slabs were poured, steel columns were erected on individual foundation pads. Threaded on the columns would be a cast steel collar which was connected to a hydraulic jack installed on the top of each column. Once the slab was poured, the steel collar became an integral part of the reinforced concrete slab. A hydraulic jack and rods would be inserted into the collar. The collar and the rods would be attached also to the hydraulic jack at the top of the column, all operated from a central control panel. The entire slab could be raised simultaneously to its proper height and then the steel collars would be welded to the column with flat steel plates. After the welding had been completed, the jack and the rods would be removed and moved to the next slab. This system was simple and eliminated all scaffolding between slabs. Photograph by Frank Lotz Miller.

Immaculate Conception Church, Marrero, Louisiana, 1957.

This beautifully detailed building received American Institute of Architects Honor Awards. The roof was a folded-plate design which was expressed on the interior of the nave, as well as on the exterior of the exposed roof. The walls were brick on the interior and also in both the interior of the church and the exterior, the brick was exposed in its natural state with deep horizontal mortar joints and vertical flush joints. The color of the brick was tan with a slight pink tint and this gave the interior of the church a soft mellow atmosphere. The only windows were the glass triangles created by the openings of the folded-plate roof. At the pristine altar on the main axis we placed a very beautiful hand-carved wooden crucifix suspended in the space. The triangle of the folded-plate roof behind the altar was tinted glass and added to the spiritual quality of the crucifix. Photographs by Frank Lotz Miller.

Our Lady Queen of Heaven Church, Lake Charles, Louisiana.

The entry was almost concealed from view. We wanted to create somewhat of a surprise when the practitioners entered the church by means of cloistered gardens. On either side of the nave were walls of glass, but privacy was provided to the enclosure by exterior solid brick walls. The landscaping of the gardens and the acknowledgment of the tall pine trees had a feeling of tranquility but related the inside to the natural beauty of the enclosed gardens on both sides of the nave.

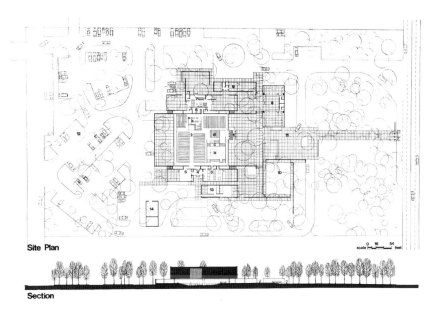

Site Plan

scale 0   16   54 feet

Section

St. Frances Cabrini Church, New Orleans, 1967.

The congregation needed seating capacity for approximately eight hundred people, and rather than a center aisle, we provided three aisles radiating from the altar as well as side aisles with the locations for the Stations of the Cross. Over the altar proper we designed a sixty-foot-tall spire resting on six supports straddling the altar and reaching up through the roof to the sky above—a very tall, graceful, thin spire constructed with a white cement finish over concrete vaults. The underside of the spire was the shape of a dome, and to enhance the most dramatic feature of the church, we planned for the space over the altar to be gold-leafed, a concept to which Archbishop Cody strongly objected, wanting to avoid criticism that too much money was being spent on the church. But we believed the feature was important to the space, so we bought the sheets of gold leaf and put them in place ourselves at night and on the weekends. The altar itself was carved from one solid block of Carrara marble imported from Italy. Above the altar we had a suspended, beautifully carved statue of Christ, not on a cross but literally floating above the altar—hands extended, robes gracefully carved as though Christ

were ascending into the spire overhead. The roof over the three seating areas was expressed three-dimensionally by a sculptural series of thin-shelled arches extending from the altar spire through the entire length of the church and out beyond the exterior walls, creating an entry canopy. These vaults, beautifully proportioned and exceedingly graceful, permitted us to incorporate a stained-glass equivalent to the "rose" window under each vault in the tradition of the classical Gothic cathedrals.

The three vaults did not touch the roof or the spire at the center, but were separated by means of a thin ribbon of stained glass, giving the illusion that the vaults were floating over the seating spaces. The stained glass was manufactured in France by the descendants of the same stained-glass craftsmen who built the stained glass windows of Chartres Cathedral. The stained glass is magnificent. The subject matter is semi-abstract, but each rose window expresses the religious theme including the Trinity, the Holy Ghost, and the Ascension. When the stained glass was shipped from Paris to New Orleans, it was so beautifully crated that not a single piece of glass needed to be repaired or replaced. It is the crowning glory of the St. Frances Cabrini Church. This wonderful church has now been demolished. Photographs by Frank Lotz Miller.

Front view of St. Frances Cabrini Church.

Entrance canopy.

Baptistry.

Davis residence, 25 Finch Street, New Orleans, 1952–53.

The first home I designed for our family was a flat-roofed, one-story, open plan. The living room had two glass walls floor to ceiling, a third wall was a solid plane of brick with a fireplace, and the fourth was natural wood cabinets with concealed storage. The inevitable interior garden was incorporated off of the dining room, and the overhead trellises in the patio permitted an opportunity to grow such semitropical plants as bougainvillea. Since the patio was shel-

tered, even with the periodic freezes the plants survived, and in fact thrived. All of the principle spaces within the house faced south, and utilizing extensive overhangs of six to eight feet, the glass walls were sheltered from direct sunlight. The house was functional and a very pleasant place to live.

Davis residence, Bamboo Road, 1956.

This home consisted of a front wing with living room, dining room, kitchen, and utility areas, and a rear wing with four bedrooms connected by a bridge that formed a floating gallery. The floor plan was actually a modified H-shape, since off the kitchen wing were a garage and equipment rooms. The design was based upon a roof approximately fifteen feet above the ground, but in order to change the volumes of the spaces, the floors were raised to different levels. In most instances they were open underneath so that the bedroom wing appeared to float in space. Extensive overhangs protected the exposed glass walls from direct sun and torrential New Orleans rains. This house was built with the construction technique known as "lift slab" that we used at Angola. A patio garden in the center of the house became one of my most cherished design features. A stream, originating in the dining patio, rambled under a raised bridge to the bedroom wing, then out into the living room garden, and finally into the open yard beyond. Photographs by Frank Lotz Miller.

Living room courtyard with stream and Japanese garden.

The house on Bamboo Road was designed with simple geometric forms. The front wing was a solid rectilinear block with the façade of solid brick facing the street. It was penetrated only by a pattern permitting ventilation to the equipment room. The brick, probably dating from the 1830s, was salvaged from a demolished residence in the French Quarter. The rear wing facing the patio was also solid brick, with walls of floor-to-ceiling glass facing the private gardens.

A few years after our house on Bamboo Road was completed, I decided that we should have a place for guests to visit and a place where one could retire for privacy away from the main house. In 1958 I designed a guest house that floated over a pond with fountains and water lilies in a very romantic setting. The guest pavilion was featured in *Time* magazine as an example of the creative innovations in whimsical architecture in the modern vernacular. Photograph by Frank Lotz Miller.

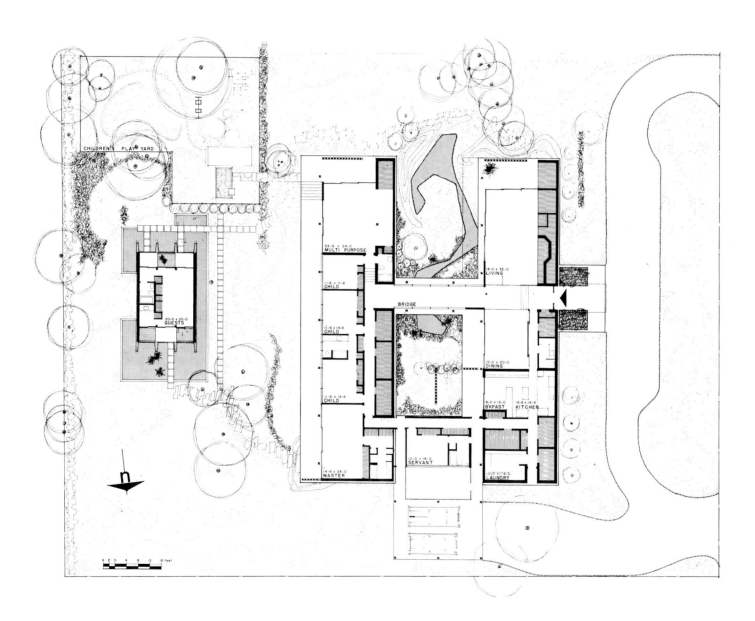

Davis cottage, 1440 Bourbon Street.

The historic original portion of this French Quarter home was constructed in the period from 1790 to 1810. After it was willed to me by a professional colleague, we added a bedroom wing, constructed of salvaged timbers originally used in a slave quarter structure at San Francisco Plantation, restoring the site to its original size.

Royal Orleans Hotel, New Orleans, 1960.

Our first hurdle planning this hotel was to obtain approval from the Vieux Carre Commission. Since this was the first hotel to be built in the French Quarter, the commission was concerned about the precedent that we might establish concerning its appearance and mass. Our original intent was to build a hotel with the flavor of the old Quarter, using traditional forms but in a contemporary way. We submitted at least four different schemes, some rather lovely ones with three levels of balconies around the entire façades, but all of our designs were rejected since they were not in accordance with the commission's concept of a traditional hotel façade. We were permitted to build no higher than seventy-five feet, which allowed us to build only a six-story structure. Finally, out of frustration, we en-

listed the assistance of architect Sam Wilson to work with us on the development of an elevation that might be acceptable to the Vieux Carre Commission. The solution that we devised was ingenious. By illusionary manipulation we created a scale that was more in keeping with three monumental stories in a more traditional French Quarter structure. We were able to accomplish this visual effect by having a very tall first floor with a balcony above with thin graceful columns supporting a continuous canopy. The second and third floors were designed with fenestration suggesting that this might be one high-ceilinged single story, and on the fourth floor we designed additional balconies with the fourth and fifth floors indicated as a single story visually. Although both levels had room windows, they were framed in a single panel, thus keeping with the illusion we were trying to achieve.

On the roof of the Royal Orleans's garage we designed a delightful swimming pool, viewing terrace, and penthouse suite, thus adding important amenities to the hotel. The first White House occupant to stay in the penthouse was President Richard Nixon. By this time the suite had many times housed Vice President Spiro Agnew, who frequently came to New Orleans to enjoy its famous cuisine. Photographs by Frank Lotz Miller.

Royal Sonesta Hotel, New Orleans.

Stanford Court, San Francisco.

This project was a conversion of an apartment house to a luxury hotel. It is located on the site of the Leland Stanford Mansion on Nob Hill.

Ramada Hotel, Cairo, Egypt.

These plans would have developed into a beautiful hotel, tall and graceful, facing the Nile river with magnificent vistas in all directions. It was one of the saddest days of my career when I learned this exciting hotel was never to be constructed. Illustration courtesy of Curtis and Davis, Architects.

Playboy Club, Los Angeles, California.

Curtis and Davis designed four Playboy Clubs—in New Orleans, St. Louis, San Francisco, and Los Angeles—that were variations of a single plan. Credit: Hedrich-Blessing.

IBM Building, Pittsburgh, 1967.

The original design was conceived in prestressed concrete. When we presented this to IBM, we were reminded that we were building in the steel town of Pittsburgh—there was no question that it should be done in steel. So we went back to the drawing board and developed an even more unique design with an exterior skin that was the structural system for the whole building with a central core also having no columns. The original concrete system that we had proposed for Pittsburgh we later used on the Louisiana National Bank. Both of these buildings were exciting creations structurally, and although different in appearance, both were developed on the principle of no columns in the exterior structural system supporting the building. Credit (bottom left): © 2002 Judith Bromley. All rights reserved.

Free University of Berlin Medical Center, 1968.

Our objective was to build a hospital with easy access, straightforward circulation patterns, and a sense of place where visitors, doctors, and staff would at all times know where they were located in this very large complex. The site allocated for the center complex was approximately fifty acres, bounded on the south by the Teltow Canal. It was in the district of Steglitz, located in the southeastern portion of West Berlin. The footprint of the building itself is approximately 900 feet long by 300 feet wide and comprises just over 5,000 rooms in all of the departments, including research, outpatient,

administration, student, and beds, and auxiliary structures. On the south side of the "platfos," the German term for the base structure, we placed all of the student activities, including amphitheatres, classrooms, and student administration. On the north side, we located the hospital administration, the emergency entrance, and receiving docks for all of the material needed to operate such a major complex. The main entrance of the hospital is on the western end, with the approach from the gatehouse at the street end of the western boundaries of the site leading through an alley of trees up to the visitors' entrance and reception area of the hospital. In the very center we placed a doughnut-shaped form, housing the research on the northern half of the doughnut and the outpatient facilities on

the southern half, with the center core of the doughnut open to the sky, connected to the research and outpatient facilities for each specialty, in close proximity to the two major bed-house blocks. These structures were splayed to permit as much light and air as possible, while at the same time, keeping a short connecting link at the center spine at the main circulation corridor.

Attached to the building on the eastern end was a separate block housing the laundry, utilities, power station, and morgue. It also was tied to the main hospital block by an extension of an enclosed 600-foot-long corridor on the center axis. This central corridor was referred to by one and all as the Main Street. Adjacent to the service building on the northeast corner of the site, we located the nurses' dormitories and nursing school.

The administration wings and student facilities were located on opposite ends of the lower level. The "bed houses" floated above the lower block with two nursing stations per floor. The research and outpatient accommodations for each specialty were on the same level as the beds which for teaching and research purposes would make for a very efficient relationship. For instance, for ophthalmology, internal medicine, or surgery, the beds and the research facilities would be directly accessible although in a separate block connected by as short a link as possible. By bending the bed houses, we were able to create a much more sculptural and open feeling even though the distances were reduced to a minimum.

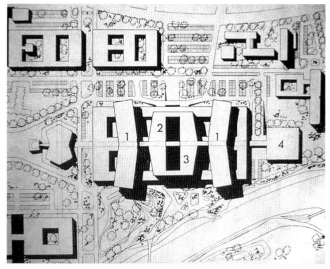

The footprint of the Berlin Klinikum was in itself a rather beautiful abstract design. The graphic interpretation of its masses became the symbol for the hospital and was used on all stationery, china, and silver, and in all instances where graphics were a part of the identification of the hospital.

Berliners have a special, somewhat cynical sense of humor and tend to give all of the public buildings nicknames, which seem to stay with them through the life of the building. This is in no way ridicule, but a kind of whimsy. Near its completion, I discovered that the Berlin Medical Teaching Center was lovingly referred to as the House of Bones. I am sure that this is inspired by the exterior screen wall which gives the impression of a series of vertical spinal columns. The Berlin Medical Teaching Center was the last of the major structures in which we used the screen extensively. The screen became a major feature of the hospital, since the lower block was 900 feet long by 600 feet wide and 30 feet high. This feature dominated the appearance and created a texture that tended to lighten the appearance of mass for such a ponderous structure. It was very effective since from a distance it appeared to be a solid mass, but as one approached the building, the shadows of the screen elements penetrated the façade, giving an illusion of a three-dimensional wall as one approached the building.

The inspiration for this kind of an approach was perhaps triggered by a trip to India, where I observed temples, highly carved and highly decorated. From a distance the very graceful silhouette of the temples was most evident and as one approached the temple, the carving came into focus and the façades of the temples were alive with activity. We attempted to create this effect in Berlin. Photographs by Frank Lotz Miller.

New Orleans Public Library, 1958.

Breaking with traditional library design, we elected to build a glass box three stories high with the closed stacks in the basement and the three upper floors penetrated by openings which not only created a spacious interior, but also permitted people on the second floor bridge or the third floor patio areas to have views into the other departments on the main level, the intermediate bridge level, and upper level. Since the closed stacks were all underground, the open stacks on the ground level were arranged in such a way as to make the search for a specific book or periodical a pleasant experience. To achieve this end, the stacks were not lined up in regimented rows but were freestanding. It was therefore possible to change the configuration of the stacks for different effects and different kinds of book displays.

On the third level of the library the glass box was carved out creating roof-top terraces, complete with trees, fountains, and open patios where, in good weather, library visitors could enjoy the outside. These patios were also enclosed in glass and were visible from the first and second levels as well.

The glass box style of the New Orleans Public Library visually related to the community and the exterior environment, but in the New Orleans climate it posed certain challenges. The glass needed to be sheltered from direct sunlight for the building to be efficiently cooled and heated. To accomplish this, we designed an aluminum sun screen, which was decorative as well as functional. Suspended approximately three feet beyond the glass wall, the screen was light and airy. In the evenings when the building was illuminated, it almost seemed to disappear. Photographs by Frank Lotz Miller.

Concordia Hotel, Aruba.

This resort was oriented toward the beach on the south side of the island. We elected to build a tall slab with a double-loaded corridor. We sloped the dividing walls between each balcony and gave every room an ocean view, avoiding vistas of the rather shabby, low-rise clutter to the north. The diagonal wall supporting the balcony gave us an ideal surface on which to add color and excitement to this rather severe vertical structure. We used Caribbean colors of soft greens, blues, and aqua to create a façade with colored slabs toward the south. From the north, the splayed walls were painted solid white. The illusion was indeed intriguing since the vista changed as one moved around the hotel from the north to the south.

Old Course Hotel, St. Andrews, Scotland.

We elected to use large slabs of native St. Andrews stone, a rough-cut gray granite indigenous to the area and the dominant building material for most of the structures in downtown St. Andrews. Every hotel room had a balcony overlooking the historic golf course. The balconies were cantilevered projections from the solid mass of the building and created an undulating façade which was a modern expression of the bay windows existing in many of the older residences of St. Andrews.

Rivergate Convention Center, New Orleans.

The Rivergate, designed to serve as a convention center and meeting site at the junction of Canal and Poydras streets downtown, near the Mississippi River, was an architectural and engineering landmark in New Orleans. Its convention halls were covered by a series of thin-shelled concrete arches, spanning 200 feet, engineered to stand with a roof thickness of only five inches. The same system, designed by the same engineers, was employed in the construction of Cabrini Church. A connecting tunnel, designed to prevent the construction of an overhead expressway proposed for the riverfront bordering the French Quarter, now serves as an office area for Harrah's Casino, built on the site after the demolition of Rivergate. Photographs by Frank Lotz Miler.

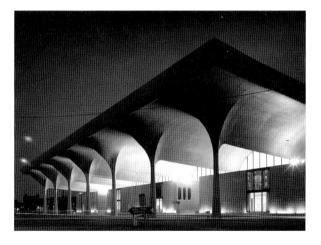

Louisiana Superdome

The roof of the Louisiana Superdome was supported by a tension ring, an innovative twelve-foot deep structural frame surrounding the building. Because this was a new concept, we carefully checked every joint in the ring structure as each panel was installed and welded to the previous panel. It was then x-rayed to be certain that all connections were sound. The sheet metal that sheathed the roof was dropped into place by helicopter. The roof was erected on twenty-six temporary towers, which were then lowered hydraulically all at the same time. This was the moment of truth: Since this procedure had never been done, there were predictions that the roof would fall straight to the floor like a pancake. Some of the people in our office suggested that Curtis and I have airline tickets to Mexico in our pockets just in case.

We weren't at all worried. As the columns were lowered and the load of the structure was transferred from the towers to the tension ring, Curtis and I were on the ground level of our building. As onlookers watched in horror, we strode out to stand under the roof. People still mention this insane performance to me today.

  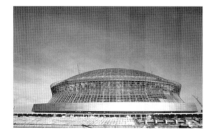

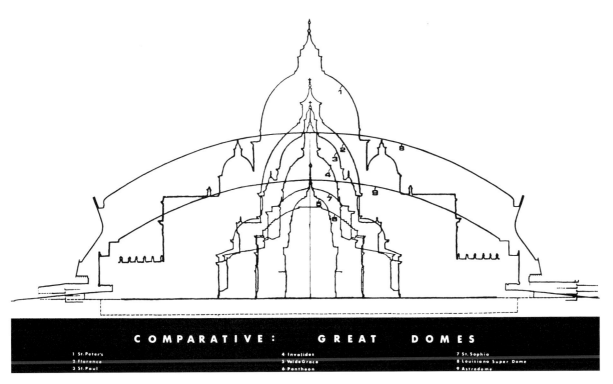

COMPARATIVE: GREAT DOMES

1 St. Peter's
2 Florence
3 St. Paul
4 Invalides
5 ValdeGrace
6 Pantheon
7 St. Sophia
8 Louisiana Super Dome
9 Astrodome

Hyatt Regency Hotel, New Orleans.

This hotel complex was built around a twenty-seven-story atrium with views across the skyline of the city, with special vistas designed to feature the adjoining Superdome. It included a 4000 seat ballroom, used for hotel meetings, as well as part of the larger Superdome complex to host large events including national conventions and Mardi Gras parties. Photographs by Frank Lotz Miller.

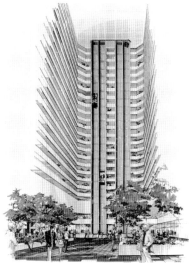

Duncan Plaza in front of the city hall, New Orleans.

The pavilion that serves as the centerpiece of this urban plaza was designed to reflect the roof and details of the historic Africa House structure at Melrose Plantation on the Cane River in Louisiana. The pavilion is surrounded by mounds with oak trees, offering spaces and opportunities for concerts and public gatherings. It was built on axis with City Hall, the Curtis and Davis–designed New Orleans Library, and nearby court buildings, with pedestrian access connecting it to the Superdome and the historic Congo Square and Armstrong Park complex adjoining the French Quarter.

University of New Orleans.

Senator Nat Kiefer New Orleans Lakefront Arena, 1983. Our final design included an olympic-sized swimming pool located under the longitudinal seating area of the arena with sufficient bleachers available for observation of major swimming events. Outside a glass wall beside the swimming pool, we provided an enclosed outdoor area for student activities. As we anticipated, the enclosure proved to be popular with students using the swimming facility as a place to sun themselves and relax between swimming events.

Under the opposite side of the longitudinal seating, a practice basketball court with six baskets could be subdivided to offer tremendous flexibility for intramural basketball. The main arena floor, which was to be used primarily for basketball, could also be used to stage musical and dramatic events as well as rodeos and ice shows. We gave particular attention to the acoustics, and such world famous artists as Neil Diamond, Linda Ronstadt, and Ray Charles have come to perform concerts.

Kuala Kencana, Indonesia.

This was a new town in Indonesia, planned and designed by my firm, to serve as a community for Freeport-McMoRan's copper and gold mining operations there. Our design included all the elements of a complete town including residences, a town square and shopping, a church, a mosque, and other facilities to accommodate a community of up to 20,000 inhabitants.

New Orleans Arena.

Photographs courtesy of New Orleans Arena Public Relations.

Davis residence, Girod Street, Warehouse District.

I have always enjoyed the use of textures and in my home on Girod Street I have storage walls of submerged pecky cypress from a lumberyard in Bogalusa, Louisiana. Throughout the unit I used different finishes and surfaces extensively. In the vestibule I have six exposed surfaces all with different textures and colors: the floor is Vermont slate, one wall is solid mirror, one wall is pine paneling, the ceiling is a painted blue sky with clouds, one wall is brick, and the last wall is two sliding panels of stained glass dividing the vestibule. I designed the stained glass walls that were manufactured in Baton Rouge. The design pays homage to Frank Lloyd Wright, and the patterns and the colors are reminiscent of some of the stained glass that he used in residential units in the Chicago area.

Epilogue

Noted New Orleans–based photographer, Richard Sexton, was commissioned by the Ogden Museum of Southern Art in the summer of 2008 to photograph a significant yet selected range of structures in New Orleans associated with the career of Arthur Q. Davis. Sexton, who has published a number of critically acclaimed architectural publications, including several on New Orleans, completed most of these photographs in late August, as the third anniversary of Hurricane Katrina approached, before Hurricane Gustav initiated another large-scale evacuation of the city.

He, like most of the residents of the city returned, then prepared to leave in the event Hurricane Ike came toward New Orleans in early September, rather than Houston and Galveston, where Ike eventually landed. The extensive wind and rain patterns associated with Ike prevented Sexton from completing the project on his established schedule. The final images are some of the most recent photographs of these sites, and reflect their current conditions, as evident in mid-September 2008.

In the three years since Hurricane Katrina, Arthur Davis, now eighty-eight years old and working from his home and office in the Warehouse Arts District of New Orleans, has been actively involved in efforts to preserve, restore, and protect the architectural legacy he and his diverse partners established over a period of six decades in the city of New Orleans. He has witnessed notable success stories, and he has seen notable losses, often played out equally on the front pages of his local newspaper, the *Times-Picayune*, as part of the ongoing political and preservation battle that marks the slow and often frustrating recovery and rebuilding process in New Orleans and along the Gulf Coast region.

Certainly one of the most important milestones for Davis, and for the city, was the reopening of the restored and remodeled Louisiana Superdome, completed at an expense of $185 million, on September 25, 2006. For those of us present on that historic day, when an iconic symbol of the city was restored to its earlier stature, reflecting the rebirth and rebuilding of a proud but battered city, it was a moment to be savored and long remembered. Words fail to describe the atmosphere that surrounded the Superdome and the surrounding urban environment that day. And, as a bonus for the long-suffering Saints fans, their team defeated longtime rivals, the Atlanta Falcons, 23-3. Arthur Davis could not have been more pleased, and the Saints continued to host a successful season in the Dome, providing inspiration for the city during the second year of recovery.

The New Orleans Arena, located next to the Superdome, and originally opened in 1999, was restored and open to public use, eventually hosting a select number of games for the hometown New Orleans Hornets basketball team, transitionally located in Oklahoma City for some time after Katrina. Eventually, the Hornets returned to New Orleans, and with a championship season, drew record crowds to sold-out games in the Arena, adding impetus to the recovery of the city, and filling the hotels and restaurants of the city with visitors (as had the Saints games). The Arena served the city in many ways after its reopening, fulfilling the original vision for the facility. Davis served as a consultant on the restoration of the Arena and the Superdome, and he celebrated the reopening of both.

Other earlier modernist projects proved to be less optimistic, especially the St. Frances Cabrini Church, located in the Gentilly neighborhood at 5500 Paris Avenue, whose preservation and future were the subject of a long public debate. The church and its adjoining school were designed in 1961 and served as a prominent focal point in one of the cities more vital postwar neighborhoods, educating a wide range of students and serving a diverse range of Catholic parishioners. After the massive flooding and destruction of the Ninth Ward and Holy Cross neighborhoods during Katrina, advocates for the rebuilding of the influential Holy Cross School selected the site of the damaged St. Frances Cabrini church and school as their preferred location, describing Holy Cross as an ideal project to bring families and students back to a devastated and slowly recovering neighborhood.

After months of public and private debate, much of it played out on television, in the newspapers, and on talk radio shows across the city—no doubt reminiscent of the Rivergate controversies of the 1990s for Davis, when preservation advocates failed to protect another modern landmark structure—the decision was made to demolish the church and school. The demolition took place in the summer of 2007, and construction of a new, and more traditional, complex for the Holy Cross School is currently underway.

The fate of two important Curtis and Davis school projects, both nationally recognized as modernist landmarks when they opened—Thomy Lafon Elementary School and George Washington Carver Junior-Senior High School—the former next to the Magnolia Housing project (now demolished) in Central City and the latter near the Industrial Canal, await decisions about their future use or demolition. While historic preservationists and modern advocates call for preserving the schools, the Louisiana Landmarks Society included both on its list of the nine most endangered historic buildings in the city. Causing added concern is the fact that both are featured on the Recovery School District's master plan that calls for their "complete replacement."

Another ongoing controversy following Katrina, related to the fate of traditional public housing in the city, focused on efforts by many officials of federal and city government to advance the planned demolition of the major housing projects across the city. The Magnolia Housing project, lo-

cated next to Thomy Lafon until earlier this year, has now been largely demolished, leaving vacant fields next to the school site. In contrast, the Guste homes project, designed as a modernist high-rise complex by the Curtis and Davis firm, continues to serve its purpose for public housing, surviving not far from the nearby Superdome and New Orleans Arena.

The attention of preservation groups and organizations such as Regional Modernism and DOCOMOMO, increasingly active in the past three years in New Orleans, have brought a new focus on the buildings such as the Automotive Life Insurance Company building at 4140 Canal Street, designed by Curtis and Davis in 1963. Its innovative use of concrete construction and its delicate columns and vaults, centering around a central entry court, make it a notable example of modernist design in the Mid-City area. Plans are reportedly being currently prepared for its preservation by a private developer.

Two residential projects, one the former home of Arthur Davis and the other an important private commission, illustrate the various states and conditions of these properties today. The former Davis house, located on Bamboo Road, notable for its open plan and the experimental construction of its innovative guest house, has been dramatically altered, the details of its modernist heritage covered beneath a new decorative façade. In contrast, the Steinberg House, located in the city's Garden District is undergoing a comprehensive preservation and restoration program, under the direction of New Orleans architect Lee Ledbetter, for current owners, John and Lynn Fishback.

Projects for Tulane University and the University of New Orleans also reflect the current conditions and status of the city's universities in the post-Katrina era. At Tulane, the Curtis and Davis–designed University Student Center has completed a major renovation and expansion program, building upon the design and concept of the earlier project, updating it for a new century while respecting its modernist roots. And at the University of New Orleans, where an original campus plan was completed by Curtis and Davis for the 1958 opening of the school, several of the original classroom buildings continue to function and appear quite like they did at the time of their opening. Additionally, as the University of New Orleans celebrates its fiftieth anniversary, the restored and renovated Nat Keifer Lakefront Arena, reopened in May of 2008, has returned to its function as a prominent part of the university's daily life and public outreach, offering a venue for a diverse range of sporting, concert, and performance events.

Superdome and New Orleans Arena.

The New Orleans Arena (left) and the Louisiana Superdome, 2008.

Dr. Martin Luther King, Jr., Boulevard, New Orleans, with the Superdome in the background.

Thomy Lafon School.

Thomy Lafon Elementary School, New Orleans, 2008. © Richard Sexton. All rights reserved.

George Washington Carver School.

The George Washington Carver Elementary, Junior, and Senior High School,
New Orleans, 2008. © Richard Sexton. All rights reserved.

Guste Housing.

Automotive Life Building.

Automotive Life Insurance building, 2008. © Richard Sexton. All rights
reserved.

Steinberg Residence.

Julian Steinberg residence, New Orleans. Originally designed by Curtis & Davis in 1958, the house is now owned by John and Lynn Fishback. © Richard Sexton. All rights reserved.

University of New Orleans.